LEGALLY STRAIGHT

CRITICAL AMERICA

General Editors: RICHARD DELGADO and JEAN STEFANCIC

Recent titles in the Critical America series include:

The First Amendment in Cross-Cultural Perspective: A Comparative Legal Analysis of the Freedom of Speech
Ronald J. Krotoszynski Jr.

Feminist Legal Theory: A Primer
Nancy Levit and
Robert R. M. Verchick

The Emergence of Mexican America: Recovering Stories of Mexican Peoplehood in U.S. Culture
John-Michael Rivera

Law and Class in America: Trends since the Cold War
Edited by Paul D. Carrington and Trina Jones

The Sense of Justice: Empathy in Law and Punishment
Markus Dirk Dubber

No Seat at the Table: How Corporate Governance and Law Keep Women Out of the Boardroom
Douglas M. Branson

White by Law: The Legal Construction of Race, Revised Edition
Ian Haney López

Opening the Floodgates: Why America Needs to Rethink Its Borders and Immigration Laws
Kevin R. Johnson

The Reproductive Rights Reader: Law, Medicine, and the Construction of Motherhood
Edited by Nancy Ehrenreich

Chicano Students and the Courts: The Mexican American Legal Struggle for Educational Equality
Richard R. Valencia

Whitewashed: America's Invisible Middle Eastern Minority
John Tehranian

Law's Detour: Justice Displaced in the Bush Administration
Peter Margulies

Citizenship and Its Exclusions: A Classical, Constitutional, and Critical Race Critique
Ediberto Román

Critical Race Theory: An Introduction, Second Edition
Richard Delgado and Jean Stefancic

Meeting the Enemy: American Exceptionalism and International Law
Natsu Taylor Saito

Getting in the Game: Title IX and the Women's Sports Revolution
Deborah L. Brake

Legally Straight: Sexuality, Childhood, and the Cultural Value of Marriage
Joe Rollins

For a complete list of titles in the series, please visit the New York University Press website at www.nyupress.org.

Legally Straight

Sexuality, Childhood, and the Cultural Value of Marriage

Joe Rollins

NEW YORK UNIVERSITY PRESS
New York

NEW YORK UNIVERSITY PRESS
New York
www.nyupress.org

ISBN: 978-0-8147-7598-1

For Library of Congress Cataloging-in-Publication data, please contact the Library of Congress.

New York University Press books are printed on acid-free paper, and their binding materials are chosen for strength and durability. We strive to use environmentally responsible suppliers and materials to the greatest extent possible in publishing our books.

Manufactured in the United States of America

10 9 8 7 6 5 4 3 2 1

Also available as an ebook

CONTENTS

ACKNOWLEDGMENTS

For better or for worse, this book has been a long time in the making, and I owe many people many thanks for supporting the project along the way. It started during a sabbatical year at the Center for the Study of Law and Society at the University of California, Berkeley, and was supported in part by a grant from the Wayne F. Placek Fund of the American Psychological Association. I am very grateful to the many people at Berkeley who encouraged me to begin the project, particularly Richard Delgado and Jean Stefancic, who introduced me to Debbie Gershenowitz, then at NYU Press. Their influence was inspirational. While in Berkeley I had the good fortune to meet Susan Bandes, who has not only influenced my conceptions of law and culture but also offered me the opportunity to present my very early thoughts about the marriage project at DePaul University. Kimberly Richman provided a similar forum at the University of San Francisco. Peter Hegarty at the University of Surrey in Guildford, United Kingdom, was a most gracious host during a second sabbatical at which time the book finally began to take shape. Clara Platter and Amy Klopfenstein at NYU Press have been models of patience, good humor, efficiency, and editorial skill. I am indebted to all.

I have also been fortunate to enjoy the support of my home institution, the City University of New York, Queens College and the Graduate Center. Chase Robinson, Louise Lennihan, and Patricia Rachal have generously provided me with the time and resources necessary to write despite the need to juggle other responsibilities. Many colleagues and friends at CUNY have offered insight and encouragement throughout, especially Christa Altenstetter, Patricia Clough, Mara Einstein, Ziva Flamhaft, Amy Herzog, Judith Kimmerling, Ros Petchesky, Joan Tronto, and Susan Woodward. Lenny Markovitz told me on more than a few occasions to "finish that damn book, already," and I thank him for both his faith in me and his insistence. Andrew Hacker is as remarkable and prolific an editor as he is a writer. I also owe deep thanks to friends and colleagues from other locations. Ann Burlein deserves immense gratitude not only for reading but for patiently listening to me think this book aloud over dinners, paintbrushes, international flights, and a bubbling cauldron. Jackie Orr's commentary is unusually incisive when she is winning at canasta. Victoria Pitts-Taylor: I couldn't have done this without you, love. Arturo Sanchez Garcia is a skilled theoretical interlocutor even in the most haunting situations. Bronwyn Stafford read the entire manuscript more than once, and aside from granting her some sort of perseverance award, I cannot thank her enough for the brilliant adjustments that only an Australian feminist could have offered. Two anonymous reviewers for NYU Press went above and beyond the call of editorial duty; I am very glad to have had their wise and generous counsel as the project neared completion.

Various pieces of this book have received valuable feedback from panelists and audiences at conferences over the years, especially those at the Law and Society Meetings; the meetings of the International Association for the Study of Society, Culture, and Sexuality; the Cultural Studies Association meetings; and the International Academic Forum. Bits and pieces of my thinking from this book have been developed and published elsewhere, in *Politics & Gender* and *Sexuality & Culture.*

Teaching is, without a doubt, my favorite part of what I do for a living, and I have been exceptionally fortunate to read, teach, and think with some very talented students. Taylor Owen Ramsey proved invaluable as a research assistant, and her keen insights in my courses helped sharpen my arguments along the way. She, along with Flannery Amdahl, Jeff Broxmeyer, and Joanna Tice, was brave enough to sign up for my course "Sexuality, Childhood, and Film"; these students' influence in that setting has improved this book.

No book, of course, is ever completed without the love and support of friends and family. My sister, Sami Rollins, and my niece and nephew, Stephanie and Aaron Ellison, have provided me with the caring foundation I needed to persevere. Jeff Faustman's steadfast patience and sound advice in all matters buoyed my optimism most Fridays at 6:00 p.m. Juan Martinez provided laughter and the world's greatest meatloaf whenever the going got tough. Michael de Coca and Jimmy Shaw welcomed me to Madrid and made it my second home and the writing sanctuary where I finally found the space and peace to finish the manuscript. (Muchas gracias, tambien, a mis amigos a Pan Adoré! en Madrid por los desayunos en los ultimos momentos de escribir.) My husband, Giovanni Quinche, showed up just when I needed him most, making me smile, teaching me to be gracious, and opening up new possibilities for a future I wasn't expecting. Across time and distance, there is always Christine Kaufman, who has taught me more about friendship and feminism than anyone I know.

* * *

Finally, I dedicate this book to my mother, Nina Rollins. Her passion for life, learning, and teaching are imprinted indelibly on this book and everything else I do.

Introduction

Marital Business

Marriage is not what it used to be, and that is a good thing.

A search for the word "marriage" among books sold by one of the world's largest online venues—Amazon.com—yields 223,270 results. A surprisingly large number of the first 100 offerings are aimed at readers whose marriages are failing. These selections give readers information on how to improve or save their marriages through a dizzying array of techniques. Some offer sensible advice, such as how to identify what is wrong in order to fix it, or how to work toward better financial management. Other authors assert that ailing marriages might be repaired through prayer or counseling. Some take aim at more intimate sources of trouble and offer tips for reigniting lost passion or, as one author prefers, for turning your wife into a sex slave. A search for the word "wedding" yields 78,453 titles, and the majority of the first 100 hits in this search are how-to guides: how to organize and plan a wedding; how to master wedding etiquette; how to make a jaw-dropping centerpiece; how to select just the right dress for your body type. By contrast, a search for the word "divorce" yields a mere 39,581 titles. In this category, the first 100 titles suggest that authors are most eager to share their insights on how to get through divorce with as little pain and suffering as possible, and the pains they invoke are not just emotional but also financial and legal. Among the most notable aspects of these books is a repeated emphasis on children. Writers offer readers volumes of information about how to divorce successfully and with minimal damage to the emotional well-being of their offspring: how to tell kids about divorcing parents; how to navigate shared custody arrangements; how to approach the possibility of new stepparents.

At the risk of overstating the value of an unscientific, haphazard survey, we should nonetheless pause to notice that it illuminates some interesting trends. Of these three searches taken together, "marriage" by itself garners 66 percent of the published titles. "Wedding" garners 23 percent, and "divorce" 11 percent. Perhaps more important, the recurring themes identified among the titles suggest some things about marriage that we ought to consider. Weddings, it seems, must be done right, and all elements—etiquette, decor, organization, timelines, seasonal variation, tuxedos, and dresses, dresses, dresses—must be taken into account in order for a wedding to be a success. But the success of a wedding and the success of a marriage are only marginally related, if at all. According to the publishing industry, weddings are fun, but marriage is among the most important and momentous things in life, and as we are told with great frequency, it is hard work. As such, it is worth fighting for, saving, modifying, adjusting, tailoring, and praying for, all in the hope of preservation. Divorce, in contrast, is to be avoided. It is painful, devastating, expensive, difficult for parents, and damaging to children.

In a series of articles entitled "The Past, Present and Future of the Wedding Industry," Matt Douglas, Founder and CEO of Punchbowl, Inc., offers an interesting analysis of how digital innovation is influencing the wedding industry. According to statistics cited in the piece, approximately 250,000 people get married each year in the United States. Roughly 1 million Americans are employed in the wedding industry, which, in economic terms, is worth approximately $60 billion in the United States alone and $300 billion globally.[1] That means that although Americans make up about 5 percent of the global population, we are contributing 20 percent to the global wedding economy. Moreover, Douglas notes that although the marriage rate in the United States seems to be declining, the industry continues to grow at a rate of about 2 percent annually. Weddings, it seems, have a bright future even if marriage may not.

Marriage is a continual source of anxiety for a number of reasons. One commonly hears, for example, that in the United States half of all marriages end in divorce, but that statistic seems to unravel under closer scrutiny. A report published recently by the Pew Charitable Trusts notes that the percentage of people between the ages of twenty and thirty-four who have never married has risen sharply since 2000 alone.[2] A report by the *New York Times*, published in 2014, notes that the divorce rate did rise during the 1970s and 1980s, a trend the author attributes to the feminist movement. Increased protection for women's reproductive rights and greater numbers of women pursuing professional careers may have inspired the rise of divorce in the 1970s and 1980s, but it seems the trend has reversed course in recent years. People who married in the 1990s and later seem to be staying married at higher rates. The author offers some intriguing explanations for the reversal. Perhaps the primary reason that divorce rates are falling is because fewer people are getting married, and those who do marry are waiting until they are older and more financially secure before they take the plunge. Quoting from scholarly work on the longevity of marriage, the author notes that people used to get married in order to find a good homemaker or a good breadwinner. Today, according to the author, more people wait to get married until they find their ideal "soul mate," a shift that suggests that traditional gender roles have become less important to straight marriages.[3] Nonetheless, as my quick search on Amazon indicates, anxiety about the threats to the cultural value of marriage and its genderedness persists.

If there is any consistency to be found in the history of marriage, it is that it is always evolving and, simultaneously, has a long history of being perceived as an institution in crisis, threatened and waning in importance. Threatened by forces both from within and external to the marital couple, anxieties about change and crisis are intimately connected. Indeed, it is fear of change that inspires this sense of perpetual crisis. Throughout history marriage served a variety of social purposes, including the formation political alliances; uniting families and estates; providing for the orderly transmission of property between generations; and regulating paternity, child care, and custody. It provided a foundation for the family by setting up the legal fiction that families are a private entity, separate, distinct, and free from state interference. More recently, at least in the United States, the understanding of marriage has shifted from the social and political to the personal and romantic; consent is now a central feature of the decision to wed. These changes are less important to the quotidian realities of married life, and as the *Times* report mentioned earlier suggests, the importance of gender to straight marriages has been on the decline for a while. Despite being a long way from gender parity, more mothers have professional careers and more fathers participate fully in child care and the daily domestic chores necessary to the maintenance of a home. At the same time, gender has become increasingly visible and contested insofar as the gender of marriage as an *institution* is concerned. The good breadwinner and the good homemaker are no longer defined solely by gender, and yet, the growing numbers of lesbian and gay marriages around the globe are a source of considerable worry for those who claim to be maintaining ancient traditions.

Relatively speaking, the possibility that lesbian and gay couples might be legally married is a fairly new development. A few brave American couples pressed the issue politically in the early 1970s but with no success. In 2001, the Netherlands became the first country to grant marriage rights to lesbian and gay couples (although, writing as someone who lives in Spain half of the year, I have noticed some disagreement about whether it was enacted or implemented first in the Netherlands or in Spain; the Spanish like to claim victory on this point). Since that time, more than twenty countries have recognized the waning importance of gender in marriage and expanded their legal definition to include lesbian and gay couples. Moreover, as adoption and assisted reproductive technologies have proliferated, increasing numbers of lesbian and gay couples have become parents. Some nations have a history of allowing lesbians and gays to become parents, while in other countries the rights of lesbian and gay parents are strictly regulated. Gender, childbearing, child rearing, marriage, the family, and the state are no longer governed by the same social scripts that were once dominant. Change has happened globally and in a short period of time.

When the debate began, it seemed to many people almost absurd that lesbians and gays would hope to speak the sacred vows of matrimony and claim legal protection for their relationships. The Hawaiian case that sparked American interest on a national scale began in the early 1990s, not even five years after the U.S. Supreme Court opined that for gays and lesbians to claim a constitutional right to privacy was, at best, "facetious."[4] As litigants continued to advance their claims, and lesbian and gay marriage began to seem like a real possibility, conservative opponents quickly took their case to state and federal legislatures, passing laws and constitutional amendments to prevent that from happening. Meanwhile, lesbian and gay couples, parents, and families across the United States continued to insist on legal recognition. For a while it seemed that compromise would be sufficient, and jurisdictions across the country offered lesbian and gay families domestic partnerships or civil unions. Before long, however, it became clear that such compromises were insufficient for at least two reasons. First, because such laws offered a patchwork of protections, they provided only some of the benefits and obligations of marriage itself. But, more important was the symbolic value of marriage, being able to reference one's partner as "husband" or "wife." Because registering as part of a civil union or domestic partnership simply did not invoke the same level of cultural capital as is attached to marriage, litigants continued to press the case for full access, something that would be recognized by states *and* the federal government *and* would be applicable across all American legal jurisdictions.

Polls tracking the issue of lesbian and gay marriage between 2001 and 2016 indicate that sometime around 2011 opposition gave way to support. Between 2011 and 2016, support for lesbian and gay marriage steadily increased, and by the time the U.S. Supreme Court granted marriage rights to lesbians and gays on a national scale, support levels had reached 55 percent.[5] Despite the Supreme Court's ruling and increased public support, many lesbian and gay couples remain wary of what might happen given the outcome of the 2016 presidential election. According the *New York Times*, applications for marriage licenses—for gays and straights alike—in New York City surged in November and December 2016, increasing more than 23 percent from the same period the year before.[6] Similar trends are reported on a national scale, suggesting that all international couples, not just lesbians and gays, are on heightened alert about what might happen under a Trump administration that is promising mass deportations and familial disruption on an epic scale.

Legally Straight offers a critical reading of the marriage debate in American jurisprudence. The book relies on key judicial opinions in order to trace the fractures and realignments that opened in our understanding of heterosexuality as it was subjected to increased scrutiny and examination. In these texts we can see that what was once characterized as an elusive object of analysis was brought into the spotlight. As we looked closer, it seemed that marriage was becoming tarnished, and the trouble appeared to center around one very specific issue: reproduction. As opponents of lesbian and gay marriage emphasized the link between marriage and accidental pregnancy, the evidence mounted, the arguments proliferated, and resistance began to turn against itself. Heterosexuality, it seemed for a moment, was little more than a set of palliative prescriptions for the worst of human behavior. Thus it became the province of the courts to reinforce the cultural value of marriage by resisting what came to be known as the "procreation argument," the assertion that marriage exists primarily to regulate the unruly aspects of heterosexual reproduction. Writing lesbian and gay families into the law of marriage became the more appealing option.

Chapter 1, "The End of Heterosexuality?," sets up the theoretical and methodological framework that structures the rest of the book. The first section surveys feminist and queer scholarship on sexuality with an emphasis on what has been written about heterosexuality; a common theme running through the section is the elusiveness of the concept. As Hanne Blank observes, heterosexuality has turned out to be rather potent despite its surprisingly short history.[7] The second section of the chapter begins with a survey of literature on the construction of childhood with an emphasis on childhood and sexuality. Working backward across the timeline of life—from adult marriage, to childhood, to fetuses—the chapter foreshadows the end of the book and the ways that the marriage debate is part of the same set of social and political conflicts as childhood sexuality, fetuses, women's bodies, and reproductive rights. The final section of the chapter draws from sociolegal scholarship in order to schematize a method for investigating the intersection of law and culture in the marriage debate.

Chapter 2, "Old as the Book of Genesis," examines how heterosexual procreation was rhetorically positioned in early legal opinions crafted to deny marriage rights to lesbian and gay couples. The chapter begins with one of the earliest legal decisions on the issue and traces the logic of that decision into the present. In the early years, courts needed no elaborate reasoning to reject plaintiffs' claims, and thus their rulings were presented in abbreviated form with little or no detail or explanation. Excluding lesbian and gay couples from marriage required no serious effort or thought. More recent decisions are part of a different rhetorical trend, one that has required considerably more detailed explanation about the relationship between sexuality, reproduction, and childhood. What this chapter demonstrates is that the opponents of lesbian and gay marriage are more concerned with regulating gender roles and sexuality, more specifically sex, than they are about supporting the integrity of the family. Children and childhood are secondary to the overarching concern with controlling sex, gender, and reproduction.

Chapter 3, "Children by the Carload," follows the arguments about heterosexual reproduction through more recent legal opinions. These texts demonstrate that assertions about reproduction alone could not sustain prohibitions on lesbian and gay marriage. Instead, these cases evince a shift from concerns with the regulation of sex to concerns about maintaining the ideological value of marriage. Here, gender and the regulation of sex assume a lesser role in judicial rulings as children and childhood begin to take center stage. The rhetorical strategies at work in these opinions reaffirm the value of family and child rearing, and they do so, in part, by downplaying the necessity of shoring up gender roles or imposing additional restrictions on sexual behavior.

Dissenting opinions from the U.S. Supreme Court's major rulings on marriage are the focal point of chapter 4, "The Nearest Hippie." Following the lines of rhetorical logic traced through chapters 2 and 3, we can see how beliefs about reproduction shaped the opinions of the dissents. For the dissenting justices the Court's rulings in both cases signify an expansion of "We the People" that is unacceptable, a move from which they explicitly distance themselves and, indeed, represent themselves as victims of a powerful minority. Their masculine heterosexual privilege was compromised, and the dissenting justices took it personally.

The central texts of chapter 5, "A Union Unlike Any Other," are Justice Kennedy's majority opinions in the Court's two affirmative rulings on lesbian and gay marriage. Here the Court foregrounds the interests of children and childhood and reimagines the cultural value of marriage and family—a vision without the emphasis on sex and gender that we see in the dissents. Here, the recurring themes of dignity and legal recognition suture gays and lesbians to the national order, thereby avoiding the symbolic damage that would have resulted had the Supreme Court allowed existing beliefs about heterosexuality to flourish and determine the outcomes. Despite the lofty elegance of Justice Kennedy's opinions, these texts also display a preservation of heterosexual privilege, one that by minimizing the differences between lesbian/gay and straight marriages assimilates lesbians and gays into a heterosexual script and renders us legally straight.

The conclusion, "Marital Jeremiad," draws together the threads of argument from the preceding chapters in order to examine how these various elements work in other legal and cultural contexts. Contrary to the worries of many lesbian and gay marriage opponents, these successes have not undermined the operations of gender in our culture. The ongoing battle over women's reproductive rights, problems of teenage sexting, the ever-widening dragnet of prosecution for child pornography, and institutional worries about campus sexual assault and Title IX indicate that all of the most damaging and problematic operations of gender remain intact, but they have become louder and more histrionic in other ways and in other social locations. Although the battles have quieted on the marriage front, they have escalated and become more vitriolic elsewhere. New and dangerous ideas are proliferating and gaining strength in a manner that fortifies what the marriage debate set in motion. Rather than undermining heterosexuality and the marital ideology associated with it, the legal language of the lesbian and gay marriage debate has instead shored up and strengthened the social scripts associated with heterosexuality, gender, reproduction, and childhood.

1

The End of Heterosexuality?

On June 26, 2015, the U.S. Supreme Court ruled that marriage rights must be granted to lesbian and gay couples throughout the country. The Court's decision in *Obergefell v. Hodges* was heralded as a major victory after more than forty years of activism and litigation culminated in the attainment of one of the LGBT movement's primary objectives.[1] Arriving during Pride Month and on the eve of many of America's Pride parades and celebrations, the decision inspired festivity and congratulations on a monumental scale. The *New York Times* called the opinion "profound and inspiring," comparing it to other major civil rights victories such as *Brown v. Board of Education* (1954) and *Loving v. Virginia* (1967). Borrowing from Justice Kennedy's language in the opinion, the *Times* added that the Court "emphasized the dignity and equality not only of same-sex couples, but of their families and children. 'Without the recognition, stability, and predictability marriage offers,' he wrote, the children of these couples 'suffer the stigma of knowing their families are somehow lesser.'" The four dissenting justices on the Court characterized the decision rather differently. Justice Roberts's dissent compared the decision to *Dred Scott v. Sanford*, the 1857 decision holding that black people were not American citizens and *Lochner v. New York* (1905), a decision that has long been viewed as an example of judges inappropriately writing their personal preferences into public policy. Justice Scalia called the *Obergefell* decision a "judicial Putsch." The *Times* also noted that "[a]s news of the ruling came out on Friday morning, opponents of same-sex marriage struggled to fathom how the country they thought they understood could so rapidly pass them by."[2]

Many people—not just those opposed to lesbian and gay marriages—found themselves wondering how such change had happened so quickly. By comparison, the racist doctrine of "separate but equal" survived for almost sixty years before the Supreme Court overturned it. The Court's constitutional approval of sodomy laws lasted only seventeen years, and a mere twelve years after shedding their outlaw status, gays and lesbians were granted the right to marry the partner of their choosing. That the gender complementarity of marriage would be altered *at all* left oppositionists perplexed and angry, but the speed with which change occurred, as the preceding quote exemplifies, was noted across the political spectrum. Why did such a change happen so fast? There are, of course, many different ways to answer this question. We might, for example, catalog the many successes of the gay and lesbian movement not just in the law but also in society, politics, and culture. Or we might attribute it to the changing gender requirements of straight marriage as noted in the introduction. I will argue, however, that the most potent explanation for such rapid change can be found by turning attention to one of the most prominent arguments advanced by opponents of lesbian and gay marriage: the procreation argument.

The procreation argument was not a coherent set of ideas grounded in evidence and presented logically in court. It was, instead, a pastiche of half-truths and unsupportable beliefs about how heterosexuality, gender, reproduction, and marriage *should* be, normative assertions that varied among litigants, judges, and factual circumstances. While everyone would agree that only heterosexual intercourse could result in accidental pregnancy (i.e., the procreation argument in a nutshell), that fact made for an unstable foundation on which to build a structure of legal resistance. Opponents of lesbian and gay marriage scrambled to cobble together an ideological golem comprising bits and pieces and shifting degrees of emphasis in an argument endowed with particular powers but one that ultimately fell apart rather spectacularly. Legally accepting the argument would have had at least two deeply problematic effects. First, it would have compromised our nostalgic hope that formal law is coherent, predictable, logical, and just. Second, it would have badly tarnished the cultural value of marriage, sullying our romantic hopes and nostalgia. The answer, instead, was to stop resisting and to let lesbian and gay couples marry. Gays and lesbians may now enter the sacred, ancient institution with all the respect and dignity and lofty aspirations that that suggests. But that is not the end of the story. Lesbians and gays are now expected to ensconce themselves within the confining structures of a monogamous, reproductive, suburban, capitalist lifestyle. Much has been gained, much has been lost; some things have changed, some have remained the same. But in the end, what has happened is this: lesbians and gays have become legally straight.

In the 1970s, when the first brave gay and lesbian couples attempted to get married, homosexuality was viewed as antithetical to procreation and child rearing. Lesbians and gay men were officially excluded from many social institutions—notably families and schools—because they were seen as a threat to vulnerable, impressionable children; they were considered pedophiles at worst, active recruiters into the homosexual lifestyle at best. By the 1990s, as the movement toward marriage rights gathered steam and increasing numbers of lesbians and gays were forming families and raising children, opponents turned to the procreation argument in order to maintain the heterosexuality of marriage. As advanced by opponents of lesbian and gay marriage, the procreation argument goes something like this: procreation is the central, defining feature of marriage; only heterosexual couples can procreate; lesbian and gay couples cannot reproduce naturally or accidentally and therefore should not be allowed to marry. The argument focused on the one and only demonstrable difference between lesbian/gay and straight couples: their ability to procreate without assisted reproductive technologies. Litigants utilizing the argument asserted that marriage exists primarily to ameliorate the excesses of wanton heterosexuality, that is, unplanned pregnancies, abortions, and the birth of unwanted children. Although antiabortion activists care little about whether pregnant women marry or not—so long as they carry their pregnancies to term—marriage is nonetheless imagined as a necessary mechanism with which the state may establish paternity, secure economic stability, and provide a supposedly ideal setting for child rearing, one that frees the state from most obligations to care for its youngest citizens. Marriage is also imagined to be a corrective legal measure that legitimates unplanned or unwanted pregnancies, turning iron into gold. Many of these ideological positions are specious, particularly considering that the majority of women who terminate pregnancies already have children (approximately 61 percent), and although 85 percent of women who terminate pregnancies are unmarried, nearly one-third of those are in stable, cohabiting relationships.[3] Moreover, such data suggest that the primary reason women have abortions is to protect and preserve the families they already have.[4]

Gay and lesbian couples sought access to marriage for many of the same reasons that straight people do: in order to legally protect their relationships and families. Establishing legal relationships to our children and raising them successfully are goals that gays and straights have in common, but gay and lesbian couples are far less likely to experience unplanned pregnancies. Thus, it is the first term—"wanton heterosexuality"—that moved to the foreground of the marriage debate and began developing in legal discourse. Continued emphasis and ramification of the argument threatened to disrupt the social scripts through which we know and understand heterosexuality, procreation, gender, childhood and, most important, the family. Taken to its logical conclusion, the procreation argument would reduce marriage to nothing more than a palliative for the excesses of heterosexual couplings in support of the carelessly begotten children who resulted from them. The procreation argument thus foreshadowed the end of romance as we know it, threatened to interrupt the developmental narratives through which people make sense of their lives, and contained the potential to shatter our conceptions of the family especially insofar as it is a site for proper gender training. Courts were left with two options: allow gays and lesbians to marry or risk tarnishing the archetypal family ideal. Despite what we think we know about heterosexuality, it appears that the concept is rather opaque and difficult to analyze. Nevertheless, because the marriage debate has unsettled the relationship of gender to marriage, heterosexuality deserves to be reconsidered.

Heterosexuality Reconsidered

The belief that heterosexuality is natural, innate, healthy, and normal while homosexuality is an unnatural, filthy habit forced on children by others is now outdated—for many people—and the illogical contradictions of such thinking are undeniable. What has remained opaque, however, are the inner workings of heterosexuality. Homosexuality may be a choice, but if it is, so is heterosexuality. Either option would be fine, really, if we set aside our preferences for social hierarchy, but that seems difficult for many. When we examine sexuality more closely, we can see that it contains so much more than a gendered script for successful heterosexual development that leads to marital procreation. Legal scholar

Katherine Franke has observed that "to call something sexual is, in one moment, to say too much and not enough about the meaning of the practice so named." Franke's critique draws evidence from three sources: the ritualized semen practices of the Sambians, a community of people in Papua New Guinea where boys are required to fellate their elders from a very young age; the assault on Abner Louima, whom New York City police officers sodomized with the wooden handle of a toilet plunger; and the well-orchestrated rapes of Croatian and Muslim women during the war in Yugoslavia. Labeling the practices of the Sambians or the brutality of the NYPD as sexual, Franke argues, overlooks the other forms of social power that are at work in each case. In the case of the Sambians, the ritualized practices that Western anthropologists were quick to call sexual were, in fact, neither erotic nor reproductive (what Westerners might consider sexual) but were part of a set of cultural practices that reinforced sexism by constructing women as unclean, a threat to virility and masculinity, and inferior to men. Similarly, the assault on Abner Louima was less sexual than it was about the racism of the NYPD. Instead, Franke proposes, we would do well to consider the approach taken by the International Tribunal for the Prosecution of Persons Responsible for Serious Violations of International Humanitarian Law Committed in the Territory of the Former Yugoslavia since 1991 (the ICTY). The ICTY, in its prosecution of rapists, "treated sex-related violence as a serious, and often grave, breach of international humanitarian law, while avoiding the mistake of essentializing sexual conduct as a special kind of injury that deserves to be 'protected, surrounded, invested' with a unique legal response." As Franke insists, the issue is not how to define sex or how to punish sexual transgression but how to recognize sex as but one type of bodily act that may serve ends *other than* eros or reproduction.[5]

In the United States we tend to think of heterosexuality as defined by two constitutive elements: sexual attraction between bodies that are differently gendered and the reproductive potential of such unions. The elusiveness of heterosexuality as an object of critique is aptly illustrated by quotations from two scholarly works written fifteen years apart. As Adrienne Rich observed:

> The assumption that "most women are innately heterosexual" stands as a theoretical and political stumbling block for many women. It remains a

> tenable assumption, partly because lesbian existence has been written out of history or catalogued under disease; partly because it has been treated as exceptional rather than intrinsic; partly because to acknowledge that for women heterosexuality may not be a "preference" at all but something that has had to be imposed, managed, organized, propagandized and maintained by force is an immense step to take if you consider yourself freely and "innately" heterosexual. Yet the failure to examine heterosexuality as an institution is like failing to admit that the economic system called capitalism or the caste system of racism is maintained by a variety of forces, including both physical violence and false consciousness.[6]

Fifteen years later Jonathan Ned Katz wrote:

> The intimidating notion that heterosexuality refers to everything differently sexed and gendered and eroticized is, it turns out, one of the conceptual dodges that keeps heterosexuality from becoming the focus of sustained, critical analysis. You can't analyze everything.[7]

What is striking about these passages is that they call for greater attention to the inner workings of heterosexuality, and still the concept remains so deeply embedded in our consciousness as necessary to survival of the human species that it continues to evade scrutiny. Katz continues, observing that "[h]eterosexuality, we usually assume, is as old as procreation, as ancient as the lust of the fallen Eve and Adam, as eternal as the sex and gender difference of that first lady and initial gentleman."[8]

As Katz argues, heterosexuality—that is, the origins of the word itself—can be traced to the early sexologists for whom it meant something very different from what we understand today. In its first iteration, appearing in the work of Richard von Krafft-Ebing in 1893, heterosexuality (then a hyphenated term) referred to male-female sexual relations and included both eroticism and a reproductive instinct, a distinction that was briefly set aside when the concept was imported to America. In its first American usage, the word "heterosexual" seemed to refer to straight sexuality that was not intended for reproduction and, consequently, for a moment, it seemed freighted with pathological potential; people were having sex just for fun. Heterosexuality, in this usage, referred to too much straight sex without enough babies. But use of the term to signify pathology or deviance was short-lived, and before long the terms "heterosexual" and "homosexual" "helped to make sex difference and eros the basic distinguishing features of a new linguistic, conceptual, and social ordering of desire." Katz goes on to argue that heterosexuality "is invented in discourse as that which is outside discourse. It's manufactured in a particular discourse as that which is universal. It's constructed in a historically specific discourse as that which is outside time. It was constructed quite recently as that which is very old: Heterosexuality is an invented tradition."[9]

Several prominent scholars across the twentieth century helped invent the system of sexuality we now see dominating mainstream American thought. Among those, Sigmund Freud was one of the most prominent, and critiques of his work have ranged across a spectrum of possibility, with many emphasizing how his particular brand of heterosexuality has been linked to gender oppression.[10] But as John Gagnon and William Simon pointed out, Freud, as well as Alfred Kinsey—another of the most prominent sexologists of the twentieth century—assumed that sexuality was a natural, instinctive drive and one that was anchored in the body, a perspective that overlooked the social roles and meanings attributed to sexual behavior. According to Gagnon and Simon:

> It is this assembly of the reality of the body and the social and cultural sources of attributed meaning that is missing in the two greatest modern students of sexuality in the West. In Freud we find a world dominated by the search for motivation, a world in which the body never seems to be very problematic since it is both the source of naturalness (anatomy becomes destiny) and the passive recipient of meanings attributed to it. . . . In the work of Kinsey we see the opposite thrust. Here we have sexual women and men in the decorticated state; the bodies arrange themselves, orgasm occurs, one counts it seeking a continuum of rates where normalcy is a function of location on a distribution scale.[11]

These "natural" conceptions of sexuality as located in the body and devoid of social content guided much of the scholarship on sexuality in the twentieth century. Early attempts to explore this system and deconstruct heterosexuality began in the 1970s as radical and socialist feminists began to unpack the links between heterosexuality and gender inequality.[12]

At the time that heterosexuality became the dominant paradigm organizing our sexual lives, it served as the glue that reinforced a number of other social structures. It evolved as a script whereby men were economically tied to the women they impregnated, women were made dependent upon the support of those men, and communities relied on marriage to delineate the proper boundaries of the basic economic unit known as the family and to know who properly belonged within each unit. Because heterosexuality established an ostensibly "natural" set of boundaries around the legally, socially, politically, and economically necessary cluster of people we know as family, the fact of its invention went largely unnoticed outside of scholarly circles; it is assumed to have originated in a social ordering of the world that was ordained by nature, God, or some other immutable force. Because of the biological realities of childbearing, this conception of family came to be thought of as a natural structure that located women's unpaid labor in the home, made women the primary caretakers of children and providers of their early education and socialization, and set up a situation wherein men would have nearly exclusive sexual access to the women (and anyone else) who occupied their domain. This mythical vision of the family, headed by a man to whom a woman was subordinate and answerable, regulated not only gender but also race, citizenship, and economics while working in concert with other institutions such as religion, psychiatry, and medicine.

Adrienne Rich's essay quoted earlier, "Compulsory Heterosexuality and Lesbian Existence," argues that the assumptions that women are "innately sexually oriented toward men" and "that the lesbian choice is simply an acting-out of bitterness toward men" are "widely current in literature and in the social sciences." She continues:

> I am concerned here with two other matters as well: first, how and why women's choice of women as passionate comrades, life partners, coworkers, lovers, tribe, has been crushed, invalidated, forced into hiding and disguise; and second, the virtual or total neglect of lesbian existence in a wide range of writings, including feminist scholarship. Obviously there is a connection here. I believe that much feminist theory and criticism is stranded on this shoal.[13]

A primary objective of Rich's essay is to show that feminist scholarship of the time had paid little attention to the wider system of sexuality, specifically heterosexuality, the invisibility of lesbians, and the ways the two constructs relate to gender oppression. Monique Wittig offered an important contribution in her essay "The Straight Mind," which concludes with a striking claim: "Lesbians are not women."[14] Sociologist Steven Seidman summarizes these debates by observing that in her essay "Thinking Sex," Gayle Rubin offered a radical theory of sex intended to "denounce erotic injustice and sexual oppression" by heuristically distinguishing sexuality and gender, unlike Rich and Wittig, for whom gender oppression and the regulation of sexuality were more closely linked.[15] Although Rubin sees the two systems as connected, her insistence on treating them as analytically separate marked an important shift in the literatures of both feminism and sexuality.

Rubin began by observing that "several persistent features of thought about sex inhibit the development" of theory that might allow us to disentangle sexuality and gender oppression. The inhibitions she identified include six key elements. The first is sexual essentialism, or "the idea that sex is a natural force that exists prior to social life and shapes institutions." Sex negativity is the belief that sex is a "dangerous, destructive, negative force." Sexuality is also marked by a fallacy of misplaced scale by which sexual acts are "burdened with an excess of significance." To borrow Rubin's example, other preferences linked to bodily acts are socially acceptable, such as a preference for spicy food; variations in sexual preferences are not accepted so easily as value-free. A hierarchical valuation of sex acts places "[m]arital, reproductive heterosexuals" alone "at the top of the erotic pyramid." What Rubin called the domino theory of sexual peril encompasses the belief that if anything changes within the current system the "barrier against scary sex will crumble and something unspeakable will skitter across"; this slippery slope narrative was seen frequently in arguments opposed to lesbian and gay marriage. If gays and lesbians are allowed to marry, opponents argue, people will begin making arguments in favor of incestuous, interspecies, and intergenerational marriages, too. The lack of a concept of benign sexual variation makes it difficult if not impossible to imagine that sexuality might operate differently. Rubin summarizes: "One of the most tenacious ideas about sex is that there is one best way to do it, and that everyone should do it that way."[16]

Within her schematizing of these elements, Rubin enumerated the criteria by which sexual acts are given value or cast into the realm of deviance. At the top of her erotic pyramid, sexual acts are deemed to be good, normal, and natural if they are "heterosexual, marital, monogamous, reproductive, and non-commercial." They should also be "coupled [i.e., not alone or in groups], relational [as opposed to anonymous], within the same generation, and occur at home. [They] should not involve pornography, fetish objects, sex toys of any sort, or roles other than male or female" (i.e., vanilla). "Bad sex," in contrast, "may be homosexual, unmarried, promiscuous, non-procreative, or commercial. It may be masturbatory or take place at orgies, may be casual, may cross generational lines, and may take place in 'public,' or at least in the bushes or the baths. It may involve the use of pornography, fetish objects, sex toys, or unusual roles."[17]

Rubin's insights offered a set of heuristic tools for imagining a different sexual system, one with potential to free people from the harsh regulation of sex that is codified in law; pathologized in science, medicine, and psychology; and made sinful in religion. Throughout the twentieth century, heterosexuality and homosexuality served as the prominent markers of good and bad sex, respectively. Heterosexuality was thought of as the conceptually pure rubric that contained everything of sexual value. Homosexuality, meanwhile, was the catchall proxy for all forms of sexual deviance and degeneracy. Gays and lesbians were assumed to be promiscuous pedophiles, committed to sexual perversion, and incapable of reproduction. Because heterosexuals were good sexual citizens, they were allowed to marry (and divorce), with decreasing levels of state regulation. Lesbian and gay couples, however, were criminalized and denied marriage rights. In the debate over marriage rights for lesbian and gay couples, the arrangement of these value markers gave rise to a chicken-and-egg sort of conundrum: Are gays and lesbians properly denied marriage because they are practitioners of bad sex, or are gays and lesbians bad sexual citizens because they are denied access to the taming institution of marriage?

As historians John D'Emilio and Estelle Freedman point out, the distinction between sexual ideology (what ought to be) and sexual behavior (what is) has often provided the framework guiding studies of sexuality. Researchers of sexuality adopted a particular sexual ideology, one guided by unstated assumptions and showing that that ideology differs significantly from the reality of how most people actually conduct their sex lives. Two examples will serve to illustrate the point. When Alfred Kinsey published *Sexual Behavior in the Human Male* in 1948, the public was titillated to learn that men actually have sex in very creative ways involving a wider variety of partners and practices than had been previously assumed. Kinsey's work was widely heralded, and he became something of a media sensation in his time. When he published *Sexual Behavior in the Human Female* in 1953, his findings showed that women were also more adventurous in their sexual behavior than the public had previously recognized. Reception of this latter work was not nearly so warm; in fact, readers were outraged to have had their ideological assumptions about women disrupted. Sexual licentiousness among men was entertaining; sexual licentiousness among women was horrifying. Martha Nussbaum's *From Disgust to Humanity* provides another example. Nussbaum begins her book with an epigraph borrowed from antigay crusader Paul Cameron, and the passage chosen casts gay male sexuality in terms of virulent disgust: "The typical sexual practices of homosexuals are a medical horror story—imagine exchanging saliva, feces, semen and/or blood with dozens of different men each year. Imagine drinking urine, ingesting feces and experiencing rectal trauma on a regular basis."[18] Nussbaum correctly observes that antigay animus is often cast in terms of disgust, and she also points out that the sexual practices of heterosexuals are just as often disgusting. What Nussbaum misses, however, is the friction that results when an ideology of antigay disgust rubs against homoerotic desire. Presumptively straight men often have sex with other straight men, and the desire for such homoerotic bonding motivates, indeed demands, expressions of disgust in order to shore up what Laud Humphreys called the "breastplate of righteousness."[19] Disgust fortifies the transgressor's armor and is performed for the purpose of denying, deflecting, and relocating the threatening taint of gay desire.

To deepen our understanding of the relationship between ideology and behavior, D'Emilio and Freedman offer three suggestions for what we must attend: the changing meaning of sexual acts, the regulation of sexuality, and sexual politics. As their book makes clear, "the dominant meaning of sexuality has changed during our history from a primary association with reproduction within families to a primary association with emotional intimacy and physical pleasure for individuals." Second, as they document, the system of sexual regulation has changed, too. Whereas the family was the primary site of sexual regulation during America's early history, the roles of the church, the state, and medicine have waxed and waned across the past two centuries. In the late twentieth century, sexual regulation remained a concern for each of these institutions, but conflict over state power, its proper role in sexual regulation, and the rapid proliferation of sexual images in the media have had a profound effect on the ways that sexuality is now regulated and infused with meaning. Their third concern is with sexual politics, "especially the competition between interest groups that attempt to reshape dominant sexual meanings." Their analysis of this latter concern offers three findings of importance: political movements that attempt to change sexual meanings flourish when an older system is in disarray and a new one is forming; and the politics of sexuality have been consistently linked to inequalities of gender; sexual politics respond to both material and symbolic issues, becoming bound up with other social concerns, "especially those related to impurity and disorder, and it often evokes highly irrational responses." D'Emilio and Freedman's work traces sexuality across the course of American history in detail, and they provide an indispensable foundation for thinking about how heterosexuality came to dominate the meaning and value of sexual acts.[20]

Over the past decades the successes of gay rights advocates, responses to HIV/AIDS, and the domestication and commercialization of the gay community have somewhat altered the basic workings of sexual politics that D'Emilio and Freedman describe. As many scholars have demonstrated, the normalization, domestication, and commercialization of gay identity have moved homosexuality much closer to the center of Rubin's charmed inner circle, and an important part of that movement has involved shedding and disavowing associations with the markers of perversity long associated with homosexuality.[21] The trope of recruitment played on trenchant stereotypes that no longer operate as they once did. The movement for LGBT rights has distanced itself from groups like the North American Man-Boy Love Association (NAMBLA), and bathhouses and other places where men would meet for anonymous sex have been more closely regulated. The growth of the Internet and the proliferation of affordable recording technology have turned pornography from an expensive commodity monopolized by a seedy production industry into a cheap homespun amusement available to anyone. In the twenty-first century, anyone can make pornography and post it on online. Sex toys are readily available, marketed at Tupperware-style parties, and representations of sadomasochism or other forms of kink no longer inspire the same level of moral opprobrium that they once did. Additionally, and with increasing frequency, lesbian and gay couples are forming monogamous, committed relationships and raising children while straight couples are having fewer children or none at all. Moreover, not only have positive images of gay men and lesbians taken a prominent place in film and television, but formerly perverse forms of sexual expression practiced by straight couples now make regular appearances on prime-time television and are received as titillating if not banal. With these changes, Rubin's criteria for determining sexual value are no longer simply assumed to fall on one side or the other of the homo-hetero divide. Perversity is still possible, but homosexuality is no longer the harbinger of sexual rabble, and the currencies through which sexual expression is given value have changed. The new economy of sexual regulation places new boogeymen at the boundary between good and bad sex.

Because homosexuality is no longer the boundary line across which sexual values are allocated by default, and because heterosexuality is no longer a safe haven for those who want their "good" sexuality to remain unnoticed, marriage has become the marker of good sex; gays and lesbians are now shielded by its protections. Although heterosexuality is but one aspect of Rubin's sexual value system, it can also be understood as the master narrative under which many other elements of her thinking are captured. The fact that lesbian and gay couples have gained access to the institution of marriage is part of a larger set of changes that are altering the meaning of several terms in our sexual value system. These changes also require the construction of new enemies to mark the dangerous territory outside the borders of the family. Marital sex assumes and encompasses several of the elements Rubin specified. It is assumed to be monogamous, paired, relational, among members of the same generation, private, noncommercial, and procreative. Whether it includes bodies only, is vanilla, or lacks pornographic inspiration are issues that somehow become less important as the assumed privacy of the institution shields it from such intense scrutiny. As lesbian and gay couples move into this private space of marital sanctity, and the stresses of gender inequality in a post-Fordist economy continue changing the social interface of the family with the society, an equilibration is taking place among the central terms in our sexual value system.

Katz's assertion that heterosexuality is that which was "invented in discourse as that which is outside discourse" echoes Janet Halley's observation that heterosexuality is a labile term, that is, it is a remainder—that which is left over once all the deviance and pathology have been identified. Within Rubin's schematic, heterosexuality is the null hypothesis, the zero remainder of highest value that gets left over when the bad sexual rabble has been divided out. Thus, it would be more accurate, to refine Katz's formulation, to argue that heterosexuality was an accidental discovery, like penicillin or the microwave oven, something stumbled upon inadvertently that turned out to be very useful. As a result it was mass-produced and marketed profitably. Today, homosexuals occupy the sacred spaces once reserved for heterosexuals, and new alignments of power/knowledge are developing to serve the same ends. Markers of sexual deviance have been dislocated from their historical association with homosexuality. In this free-floating state they are beginning to serve as the constitutive outside against which all sexually pure, desirable families—gay and straight—are formed. They are the stuff of which new walls are made, new walls between good and bad sex. What Dennis Altman referred to as the homosexualization of America is undeniably apparent.[22]

As D'Emilio observed, "Every society needs structures for reproduction and childrearing, but the possibilities are not limited to the nuclear family." He continued: "[C]apitalism has led to the separation of sexuality from procreation."[23] Thus, what Katz, D'Emilio and Freedman, Altman, and others identify as the tension between pleasure and reproduction structured our conception of heterosexuality and the family. For much of American history, heterosexuality was a necessary assumption that made other aspects of social and political life possible. That is no longer the case. These recent changes are evidence of what Jasbir Puar calls "homonationalism." Building on Lisa Duggan's observation that neoliberal sexual politics hinges upon "the possibility of a demobilized gay constituency and a privatized, depoliticized gay culture anchored in domesticity and consumption," Puar's homonationalism brings the normalizing functions of heterosexuality and nationalism together with the newly normalized, married, lesbian or gay citizen.[24] Heteronormativity—the idea that only heterosexuality is normal—has expanded to include homonormativity, and both now reference normal sexual citizens who constitute the nation. Bound up with gender, the meaning of sexual acts, race, citizenship, age, pornography, abortion, reproduction, pleasure, desire, and affection, sexuality is taking on new meanings and shedding old ones that are no longer necessary or useful.

Queer scholarship remains focused on the outsider, the deviant, the Other; the nonwhite, nonmale, noncitizen, nonheterosexual, nonnormative, gender nonconforming, differently abled subject. Queer scholars have been giving a great deal of attention, and rightly so, to the multiple intersecting and overlapping dimensions of power, desire, and identity as they shift along boundaries, within migrations and populations, and across time.[25] The gaze of this scholarship, that is to say, the relationship between the subjects and objects of analyses, often originates with academic queers who set their sights on others like themselves who are outside the relative safety of the university. In doing so, Others are brought within the academy, and new ways of seeing and knowing proliferate and flourish, shining new light on the ways we understand marriage and the family.[26] Heterosexuality is waning in cultural dominance because there are other, better techniques and practices that do the social and heuristic work it once did. Reconstructing childhood, particularly childhood sexuality, is one of the ways that the marital fantasy of the family is now being regulated.

Before unpacking the phrase "marital fantasy," I want to offer a few caveats about what I do not mean for the term to encompass. First, I do not mean to suggest that there is no variation within the widely propagated fantasy that governs how people understand intimate relationships. All marriages and families are unique, and while the marital fantasy stands as an ideal, an archetype, the lived reality is something different entirely. Second, by using the word "fantasy," I do not mean to suggest that it is not real or that it operates only in the realm of the imagination, although I should note that that is where it does its most potent work. Third, I do not mean to imply that the marital fantasy is without utility. Contained within the fantasy are rules and guidelines that provide people with a ready-made script for negotiating important aspects of their intimate lives. Fourth, I do not intend to argue that the fantasy is unattainable. Although a minority of people live in complete accordance with all the elements of the fantasy's script, it remains an important goal that many strive to achieve. Fifth, I do not wish to imply that gays and lesbians have been conned into buying real estate in some dreamworld that they can never actually inhabit. Finally, I do not wish to disparage the deeply held desires of many people—gay or straight—to form marital bonds, become parents, and live out the fantasy to its fullest. Tracing the procreation argument through the marriage debate shows how change happened as quickly as it did, but it also illuminates important changes in our beliefs about the gender socialization of children and of our understanding of childhood. Ongoing debates about women's reproductive rights, the rights of the transgender community, child sexual abuse, sexting, and Title IX—the federal law prohibiting discrimination on the basis of sex in any federally funded educational setting—are intimately bound up with the procreation argument in ways that often go unnoticed. I will return to these conflicts in the conclusion.

What, then, is the marital fantasy, and what is it good for? In its most potent form, it is an ideal and a script for how to achieve and maintain the perfect family in a *Leave It to Beaver* style. It is a script that we are conditioned to believe in and strive for throughout our lives, one founded on the idea that there is one perfect mate in the world and that eventually we will find that person, fall in love, and live happily ever after. Moreover, the fantasy is a significant component of how we evaluate what counts as a successful life. It is a dream that brings with it promises of fulfillment—sexual, economic, parental, familial—markers of achievement and progress along an accepted arc of development. Perhaps most important, it is bound up with notions of love and romance that offer, to many, hope for finding unconditional acceptance. It is grounded in notions of permanence that provide security in an uncertain world. And, as Lee Edelman has argued, it is how we imagine that a future is possible.[27] Reconsidering childhood, particularly childhood sexuality, is necessary if we are to deepen our understanding of heterosexuality, the procreation argument, and how these operate in the domains of law and culture.

Childhood Reconsidered

In his book *Centuries of Childhood: A Social History of Family Life*, Philippe Ariès argued that childhood as we now understand it was a social construct that began to develop in the late sixteenth and early seventeenth centuries. Like heterosexuality, childhood was invented in discourse. According to Ariès, childhood was not initially thought of as a discrete phase of life marked by the very specific characteristics we attribute to it today: youth, innocence, dependency, inability. Michel Foucault's *History of Sexuality* provides another point of departure when he observes that the seventeenth century was a time when a certain frankness regarding sex was still common and sexual practices were far less cloaked in secrecy. "It was," he writes, "a time of direct gestures, shameless discourse, and open transgressions, when anatomies were shown and intermingled at will, and knowing children hung about amid the laughter of adults."[28] As Foucault proceeded to show, the eighteenth century was not a time when sexuality was repressed and hidden, as is often thought, but was, instead, a time when sex (acts) emerged into new discursive locations (medicine, law, religion), produced other sexual subjects and identities (the homosexual and, by default, the heterosexual), and became part of the regulatory mechanisms through which other social constructs (the body, the family, the citizen, the nation, the economy) became knowable. The body, its sexual capacities in particular, became an especially dense transfer point at which these other forms of social power intersected. These power transfers marked a new era, one characterized by the subjugation of singular bodies in the interests of populations, a process Foucault called "bio-power." It is this concept that drives my inquiry, especially as it implicates other more familiar concepts that speak to power relations and the regulation of bodies: eros and reproduction; gender—particularly masculinity and femininity—sexual agency, and objectification; citizenship and the nation, and how these invoke and alter our understanding of public and private.

Among the prominent features of the changing conception of childhood was the requirement of sexual innocence. Producing childhood sexual innocence became a pressing project in the late nineteenth and early twentieth centuries. Programs designed to stop childhood masturbation and worries about sexual precocity in children were institutionalized in various professions, particularly psychology.[29] Beliefs in such innocence provided a tabula rasa onto which heterosexuality could be written as a master narrative. The gender of the sexually innocent child could be shaped in childhood and directed along a particular life course. Successful gender performance would lead couples to marriage, reproduction, parenting, economic success, and eventually growing old together in retirement. This developmental narrative, however, was not universally applicable, and queer people were regularly excluded from it.[30]

Challenges to the authenticity of this particular developmental arc have been met with extreme responses, particularly when it is our construction of childhood that appears to be changing. As legal scholar Amy Adler documents, child pornography was not a category of prohibited expression until 1982, and, notably, the film at issue in the Supreme Court's initial ruling on the subject depicted young boys masturbating.[31] In the early 1970s an article published in *the Journal of Sex Research* observed that there was a dearth of information about sexual relationships between men and boys and suggested that scholars should look to representations of such relationships in literature to better grasp their significance. Toward the end of the article, the author asserted, "[A]s with homosexuality, a true picture cannot be obtained by dealing solely with those pederasts who end up in jail or the doctor's office." This picture, he concludes, must be rendered with more subtlety and detail than is made possible by criminalization. Summarizing the argument of a then recently published book by a Dutch senator and lawyer, George Parker Rossman notes that "legislation to protect children has simply made [pederasts] secretive and has turned them to crime and has tended to alienate many from a society which is hypocritical about sex in their experience." Even more revealingly, he reiterates the author's conclusion that sex offenses should be taken out of the hands of the criminal justice system and turned over to counselors and medical personnel, "not only to prevent damage to a child, but to give priority to what is redemptive to the child who has any sexual experience."[32]

By the late 1990s, it had become nearly impossible to discuss childhood sexual experiences with equanimity or objectivity. A 1998 study published by Bruce Rind, Philip Tromovitch, and Robert Bauserman in the *Psychological Bulletin* challenged the prevailing assumptions that sexual abuse of children was always harmful, was always severe in intensity, caused problems in overall psychological adjustment, and was uniform in its effects. Their study, an analysis of interviews conducted with college students who had had sexual experiences in childhood, found significant variations in the damage reported. According to their findings, men and women responded differently to childhood sexual experiences, and within those groups the child's age mattered. Additionally, the types of abuse experienced—whether incestuous or otherwise—overall familial adjustment, and the types of sexual acts experienced were also important. In short, they concluded that the "forgoing discussion does not imply that the construct CSA [child sexual abuse] should be abandoned, but only that it should be used less indiscriminately to achieve better scientific validity."[33]

The authors' call for a more nuanced and careful understanding of childhood sexual abuse set off a political firestorm. Laura Schlessinger denounced the article on her radio talk show, Representative Tom Delay of Texas joined her, and Janet Parshall, a spokesperson for the conservative Family Research Council, asserted that the article "gives pedophiles a green flag," apparently ignoring one of the study's more positive conclusions, that is, that treating all forms of sexual abuse equally was a problem "perhaps most apparent when contrasting cases such as the repeated rape of a 5-year-old girl by her father and the willing sexual involvement of a mature 15-year-old adolescent boy with an unrelated adult."[34] While some commentators recognized that the findings might also be taken as good news—not all "victims" of abuse are damaged for life—that possibility itself became the target of censorship. On July 12, 1999, the House of Representatives voted unanimously to denounce the study; subsequently, the American Psychological Association issued an apologetic statement promising to be more careful about what it published in the future.[35]

Three years later, Rind published another article with similar themes in the *Archives of Sexual Behavior*. In that study, Rind took note of variations among gay, bisexual, and heterosexual males as they described what were referred to as age-discrepant sexual relations (ADSR). Although the cases examined in that study were rhetorically distanced from the earlier work by a change in nomenclature—CSA was replaced by ADSR—the results echoed similar themes. A number of factors could still be seen as causing negative reactions—coerced as opposed to voluntary participation, childhood versus adolescent experiences, incest, family stability and socioeconomic status—but many research subjects rated their experiences as positive or very positive. As the authors summarize: "The boys in these cases were not frightened, powerless to resist, or coerced into traumatizing sex acts. Instead, the vast majority either mutually consented to the relations or actually initiated them."[36] Rind and his colleagues thus called into question a number of flawed assumptions upon which antigay and antisex conservatives rely rhetorically, most potently the trope of recruitment. Their research underscores yet again what some feminist scholars have been arguing for generations and what Foucault pointed out in his *History of Sexuality*: sex is an especially dense transfer point for relations of power and one that falls disproportionately along other lines such as age and gender. People who consent to or initiate sexual acts, a position culturally granted to men but denied women, retain a measure of power in those relationships and interpret them more positively. Such an observation belies the normative gendered expectation that men are sexual agents who should have sexual access to female bodies. It also reaffirms the argument that gender *is* dominance.[37] Preserving that power hierarchy inspired the opposition's sense of outrage. Moreover, and perhaps more problematic for antigay forces, their analysis refuted the contagion theory of homosexuality. These were young men who had apparently not been converted to homosexuality by older molesters but who, by asserting their own inherent homosexuality, exercised sexual agency by initiating relationships with older men whom they desired. The anxieties on display in these conflicts are distinctly male-centered, and for the moment I want simply to note that that should come as no surprise. I will return to a fuller discussion of this gender variation in the conclusion.

The Gordian knot of gender and sexuality, sexism and homophobia, on display here has recently been subjected to more careful, antihomophobic disentanglement. As cultural theorist and film scholar Kevin Ohi writes:

> [Q]ueers already have a bad name (precisely, that is, the name *queer*), and the queer and the child molester—who is treated as synonymous not only

> with the pedophile but with anyone who dares utter the possibility that children have desires—are demonized in similar ways and, I will argue, for similar reasons. It should then become clear that an antihomophobic project should *not* try to distance itself from pedophilia and child abuse. The energies mobilized by and against the figures of the child, the child molester, and the queer point to structures underwriting both child abuse panics and homophobia: in homophobic ideology, the molester and the queer register as analogous faults in a system of representation whose phantasmic coherence is upheld, in part, by the fetishization of childhood innocence.[38]

Ohi, like Rind and his colleagues, is careful to distinguish between the trauma of child sexual abuse and pedophilia, which is the more ambient expression of desire and may include the recognition of children's sexual desires and agency. His article proceeds to demonstrate, through a reading of films dealing with the subject, that the innocent heterosexual family is defined against both homosexuality and child abuse; the meaning of the former is stabilized and appropriately gendered by positioning the latter terms as extrafamilial threats to proper heterosexual development. Drawing from Lee Edelman's *No Future: Queer Theory and the Death Drive*, film scholar Jon Davies makes a similar observation. Also in a reading of films dealing with pedophilia, Davies observes that the child is the "'perpetual horizon' of every politic, to the point that the lives of actual children and the adults they invariable become are endangered for the benefit of an always deferred future generation."[39] Ohi's observations echo those of legal scholar Susan Bandes in her analysis of the film *Capturing the Friedmans* and the events that gave rise to the criminal prosecutions the film depicts. For Ohi, this backward-looking approach means that "sexual knowledge is the retrospective index of its occurrence"; for Bandes, looking backward for evidence to support contemporary moral panics compromises due process and the rule of law.[40] Put (perhaps too) simply, the retrospective innocence of the child is produced and maintained, however artificially, in the service of a desexualized heterosexual family whose innocence is a necessary ingredient of memory if we are to continue imagining that some idealized future for the family and justice are still possible.[41] In Davies's language this representational strategy "compels us to rethink the entire system of reproductive futurism, which is not only responsible for casting fetuses as the protagonists of American life but for infantilizing everyone."[42]

The fetal protagonist has long served as an artful proxy for the regulation of women's bodies and remains an important figure in the regulation of the family. In her pathbreaking essay "Fetal Images," Rosalind Petchesky decodes with elegant precision the ideological effects of *The Silent Scream*, showing how that film's ostensibly real-time depiction of a fetus being aborted was part of a larger cultural phenomenon that magnified and masculinized the fetus while simultaneously erasing the bodies, presence, and agency of women. Moreover, she notes, the film's genesis could be traced to an article in the *New England Journal of Medicine* claiming that ultrasounds resulted in "maternal bonding" and would thus reduce the likelihood that a woman would have an abortion after viewing images of her fetus. At that time Petchesky notes, "[T]here is no reason any woman's abortion decision should be tortured . . . [by requiring her to view a sonogram] because there is no medical rationale for requiring her to view an image of her fetus."[43] She continues, observing that abortion clinics used sonograms only to determine fetal size and placement, and that the woman herself would not see the images. Among her concluding proposals, which she described as both "modest and utopian," we find one that has fallen by the wayside in the years since. She writes: "First, we have to restore women to a central place in the pregnancy scene. To do this, we must create new images that recontextualize the fetus, that place it back into the uterus, and the uterus back into the woman's body, and her body back into its social space."[44]

Contemporary abortion politics inspire much less optimism, and the ubiquity of fetal images has continued to grow. According to NARAL Pro-Choice America, thirty-three states have enacted laws that require biased counseling requirements and mandatory delays for women seeking abortion services; courts have found only eight of these to be partially or fully unconstitutional; five states enacted such statutes in 2012 alone. Among the details these biased counseling requirements require doctors to share are the discredited claims that abortion is related to breast cancer and psychological trauma; among the more invasive proposals (some of which have been signed into law) is the requirement that a woman seeking abortion must have a sonogram, to view the fetus, listen to the heart auscultation, and endure a waiting period after viewing these test results and undergoing the procedure. Moreover, state legislatures imposed significant restrictions on women's reproductive rights, enacting more than 800 antichoice measures between 1995 and 2013. In 2013 alone, twenty-four states enacted fifty-three measures limiting women's right to choose in a number of invasive ways. Abortion clinics were regulated out of existence in large swaths of the United States, and doctors who perform abortions are made the targets of increasing state surveillance as well as violence from antiabortion activists. The Supreme Court's decision in *Whole Woman's Health v. Hellerstedt* (2016) corrected some of the more egregious aspects of this attack on women's rights, but the inauguration of President Donald Trump has inspired antiabortion activists to press for even more audacious and invasive legislation.[45]

Scholarly writing about reproductive choice trends predominantly in favor of women's rights and expresses significant concern about efforts to erode the protections promised by *Roe v. Wade* (1973). Antiabortion activists, meanwhile, are given voice in many state legislatures, and their right to protest has received considerable support in the courts. The discourses of childhood sexuality are perhaps the most fraught of all the various attempts to roll back women's reproductive rights. Much of the time, even acknowledging that children are sexual beings is a possibility that is silenced in the media as well as the law. The representational requirements and prohibitions placed on fetuses and children's sexuality contrast starkly with one another. While children's sexuality has become unrepresentable, the representation of fetuses has become compulsory even when they are unwanted. These issues—gender, marriage, reproduction, childhood—are all elements of how we know heterosexuality, and tracking their realignment is particularly crucial in this precarious political moment.

Law and Culture: A Method

Legal scholars writing about sexuality tend to emphasize procedural, technical, and constitutional arguments. As William Eskridge writes:

> One cannot interpret or apply *Lawrence* without situating it in history—not just the history of judicial review of morals legislation, as Suzanne Goldberg has done; or the history of equal protection doctrine, as Nan Hunter and Pam Karlan have done; or the history of privacy rights litigation, as Larry Tribe has done; or the history of the lesbian and gay social movement, as Miranda Oshige McGowan has done; or the history of what transpired the night of Lawrence and Garner's arrest, as Dale Carpenter has done, but also the history of traditionalist and religious responses to the lesbian and gay rights movement.[46]

Eskridge situates *Lawrence* within a history of the traditional family values movement and shows how that history, beginning with Anita Bryant's Save Our Children campaign from 1978, relied extensively on narratives of disgust and contagion in order to inspire outrage and backlash against advances made by the LGBT community.

Eskridge makes an important contribution to our understanding of how sex acts (i.e., behaviors) become sexuality (i.e., ideology), with his focus trained on the specific social valence attached to homosexuality. Like Nussbaum, he frames his analysis within a politics of the body, a politics that is primarily concerned with boundary maintenance: gays and lesbians, so the story went, do disgusting things with their bodies, violate codes of both morality and health, and should therefore be expelled from the body politic because they use their bodies in ways that are contrary to biblical (and other) edicts. Paradoxically, these disgusting uses were thought to be very appealing to children and young adults, who would, in turn, fail to assume their properly gendered roles in a reproductive heterosexual economy. Eskridge pays little attention, however, to the place of reproduction or childhood in this changing story. Throughout much of the twentieth century, antigay forces relied on particular tropes and perpetuated outdated canards that asserted that because gays and lesbians could not reproduce, they must always recruit new members—usually children—into the homosexual fold, an absurd transference of the heterosexual romantic and reproductive ideology onto gay and lesbian people. Aside from the obvious errors contained in the assertion (gays and lesbians can and do reproduce, just usually not by accident), we should also recognize that the trope of homosexual recruitment strategically distracts our attention from the operations of heterosexuality. As Duggan has argued, it is heterosexuals who most actively recruit. Bar mitzvahs and bas mitzvahs, first communions, high school proms, sweet sixteen parties, virginity balls, and a host of other ritualized performances provide gendered rehearsals that are designed to shepherd children into mature heterosexuality.

Children and childhood have long been the primary focal point of antigay legal activism. For example, in Eskridge's discussion of the failed Briggs Amendment in California, the 1978 initiative that would have banned gays and lesbians from employment in public schools, we find the following quotes: "Open homosexuality, per se, is a threat to children because its appeal is as alluring as its practice is ruinous"; "A teacher who is a known homosexual will automatically represent that way of life to young, impressionable students at a time when they are struggling with their own critical choice of sexual orientation"; "When children are constantly exposed to such homosexual role models, they may well be inclined to experiment with a life-style that could lead to disaster for themselves and, ultimately, for society as a whole." Eskridge draws from the Briggs Initiative and summarizes the logic of such antigay debates:

> A deep reason homosexuality is alluring to immature youth is that it represents the pleasure principle in its most naked form: Oral or anal sex cannot be procreative, and therefore not marital either, and its only justification is pleasure. Short-term pleasure sounds great to immature teenagers—indeed, it all but defines "adolescent" thinking and behavior—but traditionalists say adults know that pleasure is fleeting and cannot be the basis for the larger purposes God has for us. Once you are addicted to homosexuality, as the immature adolescent might be, notwithstanding his parents' best efforts, it is hard to return to the straight and narrow. And once some youth become hooked on homosexuality, it is easier for others to follow the path of alluring pleasure. Before you know it, "dishonorable passions" dominate a community.[47]

There is a lot happening in this passage, none of which assumes that sexual orientation may be innate or part of "the larger purposes God has for us." Simultaneously, it seems, homosexuality is highly pleasurable and difficult to resist; therefore, it is also potentially addictive. But the narrative arc of the passage locates that addictive pleasure at the precipice of a slippery slope that ultimately slides impressionable youth away from God's larger plans for sex: marriage and procreation, two concepts that were, at the time, inextricably linked. The linkage of these two terms—marriage and procreation—and the exclusion of sexual pleasure from that pair, is a conceptual move with a long history. In the late twentieth century the American Christian Right relied heavily on such rhetoric in support of its antigay politics; psychiatry and medicine have a long history of regulating sexual pleasure in the service of marital procreation.[48] Children have always been the primary rhetorical targets of such worries.

Since courts in Hawaii first signaled to the nation that lesbian and gay marriage could become a reality, litigants have relied on several arguments to prevent that from happening. In addition to fears about children, opponents also argued that such significant change to a fundamental social institution should happen through democratic processes and not courts; that the pace of change was happening too quickly; that allowing gays and lesbians to marry would impinge on the religious liberty of those who oppose it; that the economic costs would be too high; and that marriage is, and must be, primarily aimed at heterosexual procreation. This final argument, built on an essentialist premise of biological reality and coupled with the belief that marriage had always been a male-female institution, seemed—to its misguided proponents—to be the key ingredient in a winning strategy. Moreover, it revitalized and played into the long-standing worry about children and sexuality that Eskridge and others emphasize. Lesbian and gay couples, meanwhile, continued forming stable couples, becoming effective parents, and living the marital fantasy that had long been reserved—at least legally—for straight couples. The empirically verifiable reality of their success stood in contrast to the historical and philosophical arguments of their opponents.

As D'Emilio and Freedman propose, making sense of all this invites us to consider changes in the meaning of sexual acts, new regulations imposed on sexuality, and shifts in sexual politics. Their insights remain useful here: sexuality continues to move from a primary emphasis on procreation toward intimacy and consent between partners; the power of the state waxes while the power of other social institutions, primarily religion, wanes; the politics of sexuality remain volatile. Nonetheless, the marriage debate also offers a potent example of the reasons that sparks fly when sexual ideology encounters the reality of sexual behavior. As the marriage debate evolved in American courts, friction resulted at the intersection of law and culture.

In his book *When Law Goes Pop*, Richard Sherwin shows that where law and culture intersect, the distinctions between these two powerful forms of social ordering disappear as if they had reached the vanishing point on a painted landscape.[49] Law becomes culture, culture becomes law, and telling the two apart requires drawing on a different set of conceptual tools, theories, and methodologies.[50] In a similar vein, Austin Sarat and Jonathan Simon introduce their edited volume, *Cultural Analysis, Cultural Studies, and the Law*, with a compelling premise:

> In the academy, sociologists, political scientists, and lawyers today find themselves invoking "culture" more often at the expense of, and in response to, a sense of emergent crisis, with their own master reference like "the social," "public opinion," and "law." The cultural, in short, comes as a stand-in for interpretive grids that can no longer be effectively utilized.[51]

The cultural study of law requires us not only to think about how law produces meaning across multiple systems of signification but also to consider how other forms of signification produce law. Naomi Mezey's contribution to the volume offers a valuable way of rethinking the methods with which legal scholars approach this vanishing point. We might, she proposes, think of law *as* culture, or we might think about the power of culture over legal institutions and decision making, or we might begin with the assumption that law and culture are one and the same. Although Mezey asserts that none of these understandings is incorrect, her suggestion is to borrow from Clifford Geertz the idea of "thick description," an ethnographic method that relies on interpretation more than it does simply description; meaning overshadows description.

Mezey's suggestion invites us to consider the points of slippage, the sparking frictions that erupt when law and culture are rubbed together. She uses the example of the shootings at Columbine High School to illustrate her point. When we examine that event, Mezey insists that we not only must think about the "culture of violence" that Congress blamed and targeted when passing legislation designed to limit violence in video games and the media, juvenile justice initiatives, and the other provisions of its reactionary legislation but also take into account the ways that guns are imagined as a symbol of freedom and individuality and constitutionally protected by the Second Amendment. In that instance, culture—specifically the violence of youth culture—was invoked as the impetus for legal change but without sufficient attention to the cultural value and necessity attributed to guns. Americans see guns as symbols of strength, individuality, and safety; they are constitutionally sacred. As Mezey shows, law and culture are part of the same "economy of signification" by which guns are given meaning. Legally targeting the culture of youth violence while ignoring the positive valence of guns and gun ownership and political resistance to gun regulation more generally compromised the success of Congress's intentions.[52] Law failed because the values of a gun-obsessed culture could not be overcome. Similar friction erupted at the intersection of the law and culture of marriage, and the procreation argument was one of the resulting sparks. Some states legally banned lesbian and gay marriages, others sanctioned them, the federal government shifted from the anti- to the pro- position, and meanwhile cultural conceptions valuing marriage evolved. As Mezey insists, making sense of these changes requires a thick description of all the ways that these various dynamic elements developed.

Sociolegal scholars are often concerned with the relationship between formal law, the quotidian realities of peoples' lives, and the ways culture and meaning operate in this economy of signification.[53] But, as Kitty Calavita has shown, sometimes in moments of uncertainty, formal law sabotages the very thing it is trying to uphold. She writes:

> On issues of potential controversy, law may have the effect not of resolving the conflict nor of achieving hegemony, but of crystallizing the sides of the conflict, and even escalating it. Similarly, when a legal decision . . . references an ideological framework that is on its way to cultural extinction, that action may actually contribute to its undoing by holding (what are now perceived as) the garish features of that moral vision up to public ridicule. Rather than delegitimizing law itself, such unflattering exposure delegitimizes further the receding worldview. Although some might argue that it thus indirectly strengthens the ascendant ideology, it is by no

> means therefore "constitutive" or "hegemonic" in the usual sense. To the contrary, it undermines the very ideology the law endorses.[54]

In the marriage debate, formal law began to change the meaning and value of sexuality. There was a time when the term "heterosexuality" provided the singular script by which we knew what it meant to be a family, one comprising a father, a mother, and their naturally conceived children. It signified marital (male-female), monogamous, procreative, vanilla, paired, noncommercial sex, and it did so in a manner that put some forms of privilege and penalty beyond the reach of the state while subjecting others to heightened surveillance and regulation. As Carole Pateman showed, men's labor and economic privilege operated in the public sphere but were governed by private contract and afforded the status of privilege.[55] Meanwhile, women's bodies, reproductive and sexual labor, and responsibility for care were heavily regulated and often penalized. The marriage debate did not establish the recent changes in this larger economy of sexual regulation, but it does invite us to look more closely at the ways these various components have assumed different values and relationships to one another in a new alignment of homonormativity. For a time during the marriage debate, heterosexuality became an object of analysis and was no longer hidden; thus it could no longer do the same work it used to do. In order to resist such probing analysis, courts had to turn their attention elsewhere, to homosexuality and its potential benefits. Now, other alignments of gender, sexuality, and childhood are helping to preserve many of the same allocations of privilege and penalty. In an insightful contribution to queer scholarship, sociologist Jane Ward shows how straight, white males use sex with other straight, white males as a way to shore up their racial and gender privileges. Michael Kimmel's explorations of "guyland" show us the constructed nature of American masculinity and how it is changing. Each of these components of our system of sexual regulation can be seen at work in the procreation argument.[56]

We know how law constructs racial minorities and how it also renders whiteness (il)legible in legal discourse.[57] We know also that law is often overwhelmed by intersectionality, that is, that identity categories are regularly separated and made distinct, making it difficult if not impossible for people who are doubly marginalized to seek legal redress for their injuries.[58] In the legal materials examined here, we can see that the homosexual has become a normalized, domesticated subject/citizen who, with increasing movement into full citizenship, now enters the domestic sphere and, like heterosexuals, may build a familial foundation for the socialization of children into a neoliberal, twenty-first-century nation.[59]

2

Old as the Book of Genesis

When Minnesota's highest court decided one of the country's first gay marriage cases, *Baker v. Nelson* (1971), it denied the plaintiffs a right to marry with very few words in a brief opinion, asserting: "The institution of marriage as a union of man and woman, uniquely involving the procreation and rearing of children within a family, is as old as the book of Genesis."[1] When this statement was written, it reflected an assumption of its day, one that was rarely questioned: procreation was exclusive to straight couples, and that reality justified preserving the heterosexuality of marriage. At that time, few gay men or lesbians had children, many were estranged from their families because of their sexual orientation, and, for many, avoiding criminal prosecution was a more pressing need than garnering state recognition.[2] Much changed between the 1970s and the 1990s, and what had once been unthinkable ignited intense controversy when *Baehr v. Lewin* (1993) was decided in Hawaii. The *Baehr* decision held that denying marriage rights to lesbian and gay couples violated the state's constitution, and, until the state legislature intervened with a constitutional amendment banning such marriages, it appeared that they might become a reality.[3] By the mid-1990s, the lesbian and gay community had achieved numerous political successes and was a prominent feature on the American political landscape. More important, millions of lesbian and gay couples had become parents and were successfully raising children who came into their families through the same methods used by millions of heterosexual couples: adoption or assisted reproduction technologies.[4]

The U.S. Supreme Court's summary treatment of *Baker*, coupled with the Minnesota Supreme Court's cursory review, established a legal foundation that grounded the marriage debate for a long time. Forty years later the Court's cursory decision was regularly cited by lower courts as a precedent to deny marriage rights to lesbian and gay couples. In addition, three other cases decided by the U.S. Supreme Court have guided lower court decisions on the subject of marriage. In 1967 the Court decided *Loving v. Virginia*, striking down a Virginia law that prohibited interracial marriage. That case, decided on Fourteenth Amendment grounds, determined that such prohibitions violated the plaintiffs' fundamental right to marry as protected by the due process clause, and relied on an impermissible racial classification prohibited by the equal protection clause. Eleven years later the Court again revisited the issue of marriage and ruled in *Zablocki v. Redhail* that the fundamental right to marry could not be limited by the state. There, a Wisconsin statute provided that anyone with a minor child not in his custody would need judicial approval before getting married. That approval, the statute commanded, would be contingent upon a showing that all child support payments were up to date before the marriage could take place. Here again the Court determined that the statute violated the fundamental right to marry as protected by the due process clause. In 1987 the Court revisited the issue of marriage in *Turner v. Safley*. There, the Court struck down a policy put forward by the Missouri Department of Corrections establishing that inmates could not marry without the prior approval of the prison superintendent. Here again the Supreme Court determined that the policy violated inmates' constitutional rights protected by the Fourteenth Amendment. These cases formed the constitutional framework within which the current marriage debate unfolded.[5]

The Hawaii court's decision in *Baehr v. Lewin* reignited a controversy that had been quiet for more than two decades. Although *Baehr* did not ultimately result in marriage rights for lesbian and gay couples, the ensuing national debate became intense. Numerous states passed preemptive statutes or amended their constitutions to prevent the recognition of marriages that were not yet even happening in Hawaii. The federal government passed the Defense of Marriage Act (DOMA), denying recognition of lesbian and gay marriages by the federal government and granting states the right to refuse to recognize marriages performed in other jurisdictions. A decade lapsed between the Hawaii court's decision in *Baehr* and the Massachusetts Supreme Court ruling in *Goodridge v. Dept. of Public Health* (2003). That decision, the first of its kind, mandated marriage rights for lesbian and gay couples in that state. Another decade lapsed between the Massachusetts court's decision in *Goodridge* and the Supreme Court's decision in *United States v. Windsor* (2013) striking down relevant sections of DOMA. *Windsor* paved the way for full recognition of lesbian and gay marriage two years later in *Obergefell v. Hodges* (2015). In the period between *Goodridge* and *Windsor*, state and federal courts issued nearly 400 opinions in cases that mentioned same-sex marriage, and the stories they tell range across a spectrum of possibilities: denial of marriage licenses; custody battles between lesbian and gay parents whose relationships ended; bankruptcy proceedings; challenges to DOMA; wrongful death actions or claims for survivorship benefits, to name just a few. Often, what these cases showed was the damage caused to lesbian and gay couples for whom the denial of recognition meant an inability to settle child custody disputes, to determine equitable distributions of assets when relationships end or one partner dies, or to receive benefits afforded to heterosexual couples.[6] Other cases in the group tell stories about the political aspects of the marriage debate, such as legal actions initiated when Mayor Gavin Newsom of San Francisco, California, and Mayor Jason West of New Paltz, New York allowed lesbian and gay marriages to be performed in their cities.

The procreation argument appears frequently throughout these case opinions, and the theme of this chapter is how it was used to deny marriage rights to lesbian and gay couples. The passages selected come from both majority and dissenting opinions. While there are undoubtedly lessons to be learned by examining cases from other areas of the law, the procreation argument appears most prominently and in concentrated form in those that pivot around the specific issue of access to marriage. The decade between *Goodridge* and *Windsor* was a time of considerable instability and intense debate. Within the first two years after *Goodridge* was decided, two other rulings were issued in favor of marriage rights for lesbian and gay couples. In *Hernandez v. Robles* (2005) (*Hernandez I*), a New York trial court ruled in favor of lesbian and gay couples, but that ruling was overturned on appeal and sustained by New York's highest court (*Hernandez II* and *Hernandez III*). In *Citizens for Equal Protection v. Bruning* (2005), a Nebraska court overturned a state constitutional amendment limiting the definition of marriage to male-female couples, but that ruling did not result in marriage rights for gays and lesbians in that state. Such rulings were, at first, in the minority but as the decade lapsed, more and more courts began to rule in favor of lesbian and gay couples.

Among the cases where the procreation argument appears, three rhetorical tendencies occur. In the first group are opinions that assume such an unbreakable bond between marriage and procreation that the matter does not even invite discussion. This cluster of texts contains little material for analysis but exhibits some interesting tendencies that merit brief review. The second group contains those wherein the rational basis for the procreative exclusion is more developed. These are later cases wherein judges have explained the state's justification for marriage laws as rationally related to its interest in procreation and used that argument to exclude lesbian and gay couples. Upon closer inspection, however, we can see that this is when the opposition's argument was starting to unravel. The final group of cases are those wherein judges refute (or sometimes vitiate) the procreation argument and, usually, strike down prohibitions on lesbian and gay marriage. This latter group of cases is the subject of chapter 3.

Opponents of lesbian and gay marriage who were determined to maintain the heterosexuality of the institution began revising the procreation argument, turning it away from child rearing and back toward the moment of conception. This move had the potential to solidify the heterosexuality of marriage but at the risk of undermining some of the institution's value. Using procreation as the conceptual link that mandated heterosexual marriage and the exclusion of lesbian and gay couples began to require considerably more effort, particularly when judges and policy makers were called upon to explain why some children are to be denied its protections. Marriage, on this reading of the texts, was about sex.

The U.S. Supreme Court's earlier pronouncements that marriage is a fundamental right, protected by the due process clause regardless of a couple's intention or ability to produce children, seem to have been lost on proponents of the procreation argument. But the argument as posited by marriage opponents split marriage into the fundamental right to straight marriage, on one hand, and lesbian and gay unions, on the other. Such unions could then be defined as something else, something that was not a fundamental right. Since the Supreme Court's decision in *Lawrence v. Texas* (2003) extended a right of sexual privacy to lesbian and gay couples, some litigants argued that sexual privacy implies a right to marriage. The strategy had little success.

Many litigants challenging marriage bans did so by arguing that the prohibitions were irrational, focusing discussion on the following question: Is marriage rationally related to the state's legitimate goal of promoting a stable environment for procreation and child rearing? While most courts and litigants have agreed that it is, the question and its answer are not as simple as they used to be. When *Baker* was decided in 1971, marriage, procreation, and child rearing were assumed to be part of a single, seamless construct, one that *was* heterosexuality, and there was no need for the Court to elaborate further. As the debate developed, however, a more complex question was regularly asked: If marriage provides a stable environment for child rearing, is it rational for the state to exclude some families from its benefits? Participants in the debate thus had to consider not only the state's justification for sanctioning marriage but also its justifications for excluding some families from those protections. Initially, statutes regulating marriage passed the test of rationality, but the perception of rationality ultimately began to fracture and break under its own weight. The biological issue of *how* people become parents lessened in importance. What gained in importance was the idea that marriage should help parents perform that role effectively and provide them with the means to do it well. If the policy rationale for marriage is to produce a stable environment for raising children, it is irrational for lesbian and gay couples to be denied it. Recognizing this change but defending against its implications had the significant effect of unsettling the heterosexual narrative. In attempts to maintain the link between heterosexuality and marriage, procreation and childhood became interpretively elastic.

Arguments advanced by both sides began renegotiating the schemas or social scripts that allow us to make sense of the relationship between sexuality, childhood, and the family and to relocate ourselves within a changing set of narratives and meanings.[7] As Judith Butler noted more than a decade ago: "[S]exuality is already thought in terms of marriage and marriage is already thought as the purchase on legitimacy."[8] This legitimacy, long monopolized by married heterosexuals, expanded as the marriage debate developed. As others have shown, lesbian and gay couples rejected the stigma attached to homosexuality and began replacing it with legitimacy and cultural cachet by publicly announcing their commitment as couples, becoming parents, and making families. Accepting that gays and lesbians are entitled to enter the institution of marriage has brought about significant schematic adjustment whereby families are seen as legitimate regardless of the parents' sexual orientation.[9]

Procreative Elaborations

In the fall of 2003, after the U.S. Supreme Court handed down its decision in *Lawrence* but before the Massachusetts court decided *Goodridge*, the Arizona Court of Appeals denied relief to two men who filed suit after their application for a marriage license was rejected by officials in Maricopa County. The plaintiffs in that case, *Standhardt v. Superior Court of Arizona* (2003), argued that in *Lawrence* the U.S. Supreme Court had implicitly recognized a right to marry for lesbian and gay couples, an argument that was rather bold for its time. Indeed, Justices Kennedy and O'Connor took care to assure readers that the decriminalization of sodomy implied no such right.[10] Justice Scalia, dissenting in *Lawrence,* worried that the decision would undermine the prohibition on lesbian and gay marriage; Judge Timmer, writing for the Arizona court in *Standhardt*, reassured him that it would not.[11]

Although available precedent provided the court with all it needed to deny the plaintiffs' claims with very little rhetorical effort, the Arizona court engaged the procreation argument at length, elaborating it in a manner that ramified through several subsequent decisions. Judge Timmer's opinion reiterates the claims and citations examined in the preceding section: marriage is a timeless institution essential to the future of the species.[12] When the court turned attention to the rational basis for marriage, it expounded on the procreation argument in order to exclude lesbian and gay couples:

> The State contends it has a legitimate interest in encouraging procreation and child-rearing within the stable environment traditionally associated with marriage, and that limiting marriage to opposite-sex couples is rationally related to that interest. Essentially, the State asserts that by legally sanctioning a heterosexual relationship through marriage, thereby imposing both obligations and benefits on the couple and inserting the State in the relationship, the State communicates to parents and prospective parents that their long-term, committed relationships are uniquely

> important as a public concern. Because the State's interest in committed sexual relationships is limited to those capable of producing children, it contends it reasonably restricts marriage to opposite-sex couples.[13]

Here, the court reiterated the importance of straight marriage and announced, erroneously, that the state's interest in marriage is limited to those relationships capable of producing children: straight couples may marry regardless of their intention or ability to reproduce. Citations offered in support of the passage include not only case precedents and statutes but also two law review articles written by antigay activists Lynn Wardle and Maggie Gallagher.

As the court continued to develop the procreation argument, a split appeared in the conceptualization of marriage:

> Allowing all opposite-sex couples to enter marriage under Arizona law, regardless of their willingness or ability to procreate, does not defeat the reasonableness of the link between opposite-sex marriage, procreation, and childrearing. First, if the State excluded opposite-sex couples from marriage based on their intention or ability to procreate, the State would have to inquire about that subject before issuing a license, thereby implicating constitutionally rooted privacy concerns.[14]

Here, infertile straight couples or those that opt not to have children are excused from the state's procreation requirements on the basis of a privacy right, one that might also have been understood to apply to lesbian and gay couples in the post-*Lawrence* era. Especially notable is the court's explicit linking of three concepts: straight marriage, procreation, and child rearing. Apparently these three components stand together in the court's definition of marriage insofar as it excludes lesbian and gay couples, but the procreation and child-rearing requirements move in and out of the scene as the linkage is further developed. As is already apparent, straight marriages may occur with or without procreation, child rearing, or even sex, and the elastic quality of these terms is shielded from scrutiny by a constitutional right to privacy. But after the court acknowledged that lesbian and gay couples are also raising children (or may enjoy a right of sexual privacy), readers are offered the following:

> Indisputably, the only sexual relationship capable of producing children is one between a man and a woman. The State could reasonably decide that by encouraging opposite-sex couples to marry, thereby assuming legal and financial obligations, the children born from such relationships will have better opportunities to be nurtured and raised by two parents within long-term, committed relationships, which society has traditionally viewed as advantageous for children. Because same-sex couples cannot by themselves procreate, the State could also reasonably decide that sanctioning same-sex marriages would do little to advance the State's interest in ensuring responsible procreation within committed, long-term relationships.[15]

The court here splits procreation from child rearing in a manner that not only shields straight couples from scrutiny but also allows the court to reunite and reaffirm those terms as requirements for lesbian and gay couples. In the sentences immediately following this passage, the court recognized and acknowledged that the children of lesbians and gays may also benefit from the protections of marriage, suspending for a moment the indivisibility of the terms, but then quickly drew them back together: "But although the line drawn between couples who may marry (opposite-sex) and those who may not (same-sex) may result in some inequity for children raised by same-sex couples, such inequity is insufficient to negate the State's link between opposite-sex marriage, procreation, and child-rearing."[16] This bifurcation—between procreation and child rearing—was an ascendant theme at the time, one that eventually complicated the debate and made the procreation argument untenable. The various elements of marriage, specifically procreation, family, gender, sexuality, as well as cultural and symbolic value, were regularly split off from one another as the procreation argument developed. These elements are sometimes depicted as parts of a seamless, uniform whole, and at other times they slip away from each other to serve the rhetorical needs of the moment. Justice Cordy's dissent in *Goodridge* illustrates the utility of such conceptual slippage.

Although Judge Timmer's opinion in *Standhardt* invokes procreation as one of the deciding factors in the case, scholars writing about the procreation argument often locate its origins with Justice Cordy's dissent in *Goodridge*. Although *Goodridge* was not the first time the argument appeared in legal discourse, it was, and remains, one of the most developed examples of the procreation argument in action. Justice Cordy's use of the argument begins by looking to Supreme Court jurisprudence and finding there that the right to procreate and the right to marry are mutually interdependent: "Because same-sex couples are unable to procreate on their own, any right to marriage they may possess cannot be based on their interest in procreation, which has been essential to the Supreme Court's denomination of the right to marry as fundamental."[17] Like many other judges hearing marriage cases, Justice Cordy sorts the right to straight marriage and the right to lesbian and gay marriage into different categories; the former is fundamental, natural, and crucial to society while the latter is something new and problematic. Moreover, although Justice Cordy links the fundamental right to straight marriage and procreation, these rights are distinct from the protected constitutional rights one might enjoy as a parent: "The fact that the plaintiffs cannot marry has no bearing on their independently protected constitutional rights as parents which, as with opposite-sex parents, are limited only by their continued fitness and the best interests of their children."[18] But inasmuch as these rights are separable for lesbian and gay couples, they seem momentarily to be inseparable for straight ones: "Paramount among its many important functions, the institution of marriage has systematically provided for the regulation of heterosexual behavior, brought order to the resulting procreation, and ensured a stable family structure in which children will be reared, educated, and socialized."[19] The separation, however, is quickly qualified: "Admittedly, heterosexual intercourse, procreation, and child care are not necessarily conjoined (particularly in the modern age of widespread effective contraception and supportive social welfare programs), but an orderly society requires some mechanism for coping with the fact that sexual intercourse commonly results in pregnancy and childbirth. The institution of marriage is that mechanism."[20]

Justice Cordy's opinion is fractured throughout by an inability to decide whether marriage and procreation are necessarily linked, or if they are only necessary for straight couples. Marriage, on his reading is a fundamental social institution, but his treatment of that institution is rather unstable: "It is difficult to imagine a State purpose more important and legitimate than ensuring, promoting, and supporting an optimal social structure within which to bear and raise children. At the very least, the marriage statute continues to serve this important State purpose."[21] In the footnote associated with this passage, Justice Cordy cites a 1916 law review article to buttress his point. He writes, "It is important to distinguish the individual interests in domestic relations from the social interest in the family and marriage as social institutions." He continues: "Personal fulfillment and public celebrations or announcements of commitment have little if anything to do with the purpose of the civil marriage laws, or with a legitimate public interest that would justify them." More important is his location of procreation and childhood within the framework of marriage:

> Whereas the relationship between a mother and child is demonstratively and predictably created and recognizable through the biological process of pregnancy and childbirth, there is no corresponding process for creating a relationship between father and child. Similarly, aside from an act of heterosexual intercourse nine months prior to childbirth, there is no process for creating a relationship between a man and a woman as the parents of a particular child. The institution of marriage fills this void by formally binding the husband-father to his wife and child, and imposing on him the responsibilities of fatherhood. The alternative, a society without the institution of marriage, in which heterosexual intercourse, procreation, and child care are largely disconnected processes, would be chaotic.[22]

Justice Cordy, like many others to enter the fray after *Goodridge*, builds his argument on premises that are grounded in a rather dour view of gender, sexuality, and childhood. In his vision of the world, male sexual privilege and promiscuity as well as women's reproductive carelessness must be tempered by the state through the law of marriage. But the argument gets somewhat muddled along the way. Absent the state's restriction of marriage to heterosexuals, he suggests, heterosexual reproduction would become a disorganized mess. And while the elimination of marriage altogether might have had such an effect, it is difficult to make the logical leaps required for the passage to make sense. How, many have asked, will extending marriage rights to lesbian and gay couples undermine the links between marriage and procreation among heterosexuals? Will straight people stop getting married if gays and lesbians begin doing so?

Justice Cordy's dissent is concerned with more than the link between biological reproduction and marriage. He is also concerned about gender socialization and worries about whether or not lesbian and gay couples can provide their children with the necessary tools for proper development. He writes that lesbian and gay couples cannot "provide children with a parental authority figure of each gender"; tellingly, the example he raises in a footnote places a hypothetical boy in the custody of two lesbian mothers. Such a boy, he observes, "might invoke gender as a justification for the view that neither of his parents 'understands' him, or that they 'don't know what he is going through,' particularly if his disagreement or dissatisfaction involves some issue pertaining to sex." Lesbians, it seems on Justice Cordy's reading, lack the necessary training in masculine sexual development, something that a teenage boy requires. In his consideration of adoption by lesbian and gay couples, he notes that adoption law "presupposes that at least one of the child's biological parents is unable or unwilling, for some reason, to participate in raising the child." The scenario he has in mind seems to be one biological parent and one adoptive parent. Single parents, he notes, are allowed to adopt because the state needs more adoptive parents, but that does not mean that the legislature finds single parents to provide the optimal setting in which to raise children. The same is true, he writes, regarding lesbian and gay couples. They may provide an acceptable setting for raising children who cannot be raised by both of their biological parents, but "[t]he Legislature may rationally permit adoption by same-sex couples yet harbor reservations as to whether parenthood by same-sex couples should be affirmatively encouraged to the same extent as parenthood by the heterosexual couple whose union produced the child." Again, he is putting things together when convenient and taking them apart when his goals so require. In the end, he concludes that lesbian and gay marriage should not become a reality until there is sufficient "unanimous scientific evidence, or popular consensus, or both, that such changes can safely be made."[23]

When Indiana courts decided *Morrison v. Sadler* (2005), they had the language and logic of both Justice Cordy's dissent in *Goodridge* and the court's decision in *Standhardt* to draw from. In *Morrison*, the court examined the rationality of the marriage exclusion by asking whether lesbian and gay marriages could fulfill *all* of the state's objectives in encouraging marriage, asserting that "procreation by 'natural' reproduction may occur without any thought for the future"; that marriage may serve to "discourage unplanned, out-of-wedlock births resulting from 'casual' intercourse"; but that even when heterosexual couples get married with no intention of having children, "'accidents' do happen, or persons often change their minds about wanting to have children." In these instances the possibility of marriage "encourages them to stay together and raise a child together if there is a 'change in plans.'" These realities were recognized by the state at oral argument "when it identified the protection of unintended children resulting from heterosexual intercourse as one of the key interests in opposite-sex marriage"; marriage encourages couples to remain stable before and after having children even "if children arrive during the marriage unexpectedly."[24]

Quoting from Justice Cody's *Goodridge* dissent, Judge Barnes asserted for the Indiana court that "marriage's vital purpose in our societies is not to mandate man/woman procreation but to ameliorate its consequences"; "deliberative procreation by [assisted reproduction technology], for those dependent on it, to a not inconsiderable extent performs to society's benefit the role that marriage was designed to fill for the far greater number engaged in passion-based procreation." Gay and lesbian couples are not at "'risk' of having random and unexpected children by virtue of their ordinary sexual activities."[25] According to this logic, heterosexuals need special encouragement to provide stable environments for their children; gay and lesbian couples do not. Another passage from the opinion seems to extol the virtues of lesbian and gay couples:

> Members of a same-sex couple who wish to have a child . . . have already demonstrated their commitment to child-rearing, by virtue of the difficulty of obtaining a child through adoption or assisted reproduction, without the State necessarily having to encourage that commitment through the institution of marriage. Conversely, the "casual" intimate acts of a same-sex couple will never result in a child, but those of an opposite-sex couple can and frequently do.[26]

Near the end of the opinion, the procreation argument appears again, in accordion-like fashion, expanding to justify straight marriage and contracting as necessary to exclude lesbian and gay couples: "The plaintiffs also argue extensively that it is irrational to justify opposite-sex only marriage on procreative grounds because there is no requirement that couples wishing to marry prove their fertility or willingness to procreate, and furthermore even definitively sterile persons, such as elderly women, are allowed to marry."[27] Marriage is about encouraging "responsible procreation" among people who might otherwise do so with careless abandon.

As the marriage debate developed in American law, procreation provided the rhetorical link between marriage and heterosexuality that, it seems, was also intended to stand as a proxy for child rearing. Here, however, we can see that the procreation argument began to signify something else: male-female intercourse. Ironically, the courts in *Smelt*, *Wilson*, *Shields*, and *Standhardt* all used procreation–as–child rearing to link heterosexuality to marriage when it suited the rhetorical needs of the moment, but all did so without once using the word "intercourse." In *Standhardt* sexual acts are referenced through the term "sexual relations," but notably, a search for the word "sexual" among these opinions illuminates an interesting trend. While the phrase "sexual orientation" appears in all four opinions, sexual *acts* are referenced only in *Standhardt*. In that opinion, the term "sexual" occurs repeatedly in references to the same-gender sexual acts of the gay male litigants in *Lawrence*, but it makes limited appearances with reference to the sexual acts of straight couples: "Because the State's interest in committed sexual relationships is limited to those capable of producing children, it contends it reasonably restricts marriage to opposite-sex couples"; "Indisputably, the only sexual relationship capable of producing children is one between a man and a woman"; and, quoting lesbian and gay marriage opponent Maggie Gallagher, "The public legal union of a man and woman is designed first and foremost to protect the children that their sexual union (and that type of sexual union alone) regularly produces."[28] In each of these sentences, references to sexual acts implicitly, if not explicitly, include everyone—both homo- and heterosexual couplings—but the latter is then moved away from the corrupting possibility of carnality with reference to procreation. Looking back to the early 1970s cases of *Baker* and *Singer*, one finds no occurrence of the word "intercourse" but sees in *Singer* that straight couples not only are exempt from the expectation of reproduction but also are excused from having to have sexual relations at all.[29] By drawing the carnal act of sex into the analysis, *Standhardt* began a process that expanded in *Morrison* and beyond. As is apparent in the passages quoted earlier, the Indiana court repeatedly calls attention to the procreation argument, but in the rhetoric of that opinion, procreation becomes a proxy for heterosexual intercourse.[30] This explicit focus on coitus also appears in the pro-marriage cases, but as we will see, the effect is somewhat different.

The language of the procreation argument seen in *Standhardt* and *Morrison* echoed across a number of subsequent opinions.[31] Cites to both cases appear in *Seymour v. Holcomb* (2005), where the New York court informs readers that the state "has a legitimate interest in encouraging opposite-sex couples to enter and remain in, as far as possible, the relatively stable institution of marriage for the sake of the children who are frequently the result of sexual relations between a man and a woman." In *Samuels*, the language from *Morrison* is used once again to inform readers that marriage is unnecessary to promoting all forms of procreation, such as by adoption or assisted reproductive technologies, but that it encourages straight couples to marry because they are "the only type of couples that can reproduce on their own by engaging in sex with little or no contemplation of the consequences that might result, i.e., a child."[32]

The New Jersey court's opinion in *Lewis v. Harris* (2005) cites both *Standhardt* and *Morrison* in its refusal to grant marriage licenses to the lesbian and gay plaintiffs, relying on the procreation argument regularly. There, the claims of the lesbian and gay couples were dismissed not only because of their procreative shortcomings but also because of the important spiritual and religious significance attached to traditional marriage, interests that would be offended by the admission of lesbian and gay couples.[33] As seen often in this debate, the court concludes by noting that if lesbian and gay marriage is to be allowed in New Jersey, it should result from legislative, not judicial, action. The more elaborate discussion of marriage, and what it means, arrives in a concurring opinion. There, Judge Parrillo distinguishes the right *to* marry from the rights *of* marriage and observes that most of the latter have been provided to lesbian and gay couples by New Jersey's Domestic Partnership Act. Any deprivations, he asserts, can be remedied through litigation advanced on an ad hoc basis.[34]

The right *to* marry, however, is another matter. Drawing from *Goodridge*, Judge Parrillo notes that the marriage jurisprudence of that case had been built on "the more recent terminology of privacy, autonomy, and identity," concepts that the *Goodridge* court used to remodel the institution as arising from a "close personal relationship," recognizing "respect for individual autonomy," "the exclusive and permanent commitment of the married partners to one another," "the voluntary union of two persons as spouses to the exclusion of all others," and "at once a deeply personal commitment to another human being and a highly public celebration of ideals of mutuality, companionship intimacy, fidelity, and family." Judge Parrillo continues: "This distillation of marriage down to its pure 'close personal relationship' essence, however, strips the social institution 'of any goal or end beyond the intrinsic emotional, psychological, or sexual satisfaction which the relationship brings to the individuals involved.'" Marriage, he asserts, is so much more than just what happens between spouses. It also depends upon

> the fundamental facets of [traditional] conjugal life: the fact of sexual difference; the enormous tide of heterosexual desire in human life, the massive significance of male female bonding in human life; the procreativity of heterosexual bonding, the unique social ecology of heterosexual parenting which bonds children to their biological parents, and the rich genealogical nature of heterosexual family ties.[35]

This list inspires the concurring justice to conclude that marriage privileges procreative, heterosexual intercourse and that when the plaintiffs aver that the state imposes no obligation for married couples to procreate, "they sorely miss the point. Marriage's vital purpose is not to mandate procreation but to control or ameliorate its consequences." In this reading, marriage is a public institution provided in furtherance of a social good, an argument with which the plaintiffs agree. But, for Judge Parrillo there is still more:

> Unlike the usual contexts in which privacy and liberty interests are asserted, namely to seek protection from unwarranted governmental intrusion into matters of intimate personal concern, or to gain the right

> to engage in private conduct without criminal sanction, plaintiffs here affirmatively seek public approval of purely private behavior.[36]

Here, straight marriage is justified once again by its procreative potential, which is socially important, and the marital interests of gays and lesbians are reduced (literally) to "purely private behavior," that is, sex. Ironically, what gets lost in this spin on the procreation argument is the fact that marriage, according to writers like these, is about correcting for and concealing heterosexual intercourse, that is, "purely private behavior." For heterosexuals, then, marriage is a social institution serving the public good whether or not those unions produce children; homosexual couplings are always only about sex. Moreover, while the preceding passage emphasizes the generative possibilities of heterosexual sex and the bonding of heterosexual relationships, it implies that lesbian and gay unions may be excluded from both. Although heterosexual desire is perhaps ubiquitous, its appearance in the debate is new and part of the construct elaboration that took place during this period. The implied diminution of homosexual desire is rather ironic, since gays and lesbians—particularly gay men—have long been associated with sexual excess.[37]

New York courts have issued three opinions in the case of *Hernandez v. Robles* (2005). At the trial court level, Judge Doris Ling-Cohan upheld the claims of the lesbian and gay couples challenging the denial of a marriage license (*Hernandez I*), a decision that was overturned on appeal (*Hernandez II*). Ultimately, the state's highest court consolidated the four New York cases and ruled that the state constitution did not require marriage licenses for lesbian and gay couples (*Hernandez III*). The majority opinions in *Hernandez II* and *III* focused heavily on the lower court's usurpation of a legislative function. As seen in many of the cases discussed here, these courts split same-sex and opposite-sex marriage into two distinct rights and crafted arguments in favor of judicial restraint. Marriage, as depicted here, not only was linked to procreation but was "a function of biology, not mere legal rights."[38]

In *Hernandez II* a thorough discussion of the procreation argument was provided in a concurring opinion written by Judge Catterson, who, after a detailed discussion of the distinction between the fundamental right to straight marriage and the other unrecognized right claimed by the gay and lesbian plaintiffs, addressed the analogy to *Loving v. Virginia* (1967), which is described as "disingenuous, for several reasons":

> To elevate the issue of same sex unions to that of discrimination on the basis of race does little service to the legacy of the civil rights movement, and ignores the history of race relations in this country. How can one consider the horror of the Civil War and the majesty of the Emancipation Proclamation in the same breath as same-sex unions?[39]

Equal protection arguments require plaintiffs to draw analogies between social categories such as race, gender, and sexual orientation, but passages that push the analogy to such shrill extremes are more than simply fatuous. They not only work to deny that gays and lesbians have lived within a system of legally enforced discrimination but also imply that the community is petulant and greedy when it spotlights the problem, invoking the "special rights" strategy by which marriage for lesbian and gay couples can be seen as excessive and undeserved.[40] In its justification for maintaining the procreative link between marriage and heterosexuality, the concurring opinion cites extensively the language from *Morrison* quoted earlier in this chapter. In sum, natural procreation may occur "with no foresight or planning." Lesbian and gay couples demonstrate commitment as parents because adoption and assisted reproductive technologies are costly and time-consuming; straight couples need only "one instance of sexual intercourse" in order to have children. Lesbian and gay marriage would do nothing to further the state's interest in providing for the results of "*unintended* procreation from sexual intercourse."[41] Here again, as in *Morrison*, marriage takes on a palliative role, solving the problem of unprotected heterosexual intercourse; lesbian and gay couples are above the problem and need no such remedy.

The majority opinion in *Hernandez III* relies on the procreation argument as well, asserting that there are at least two reasons why the legislature could rationally restrict marriage to straight couples:

> First, the Legislature could rationally decide that, for the welfare of children, it is more important to promote stability, and to avoid instability, in opposite-sex than in same-sex relationships. Heterosexual intercourse has a natural tendency to lead to the birth of children; homosexual in-

> tercourse does not. Despite the advances of science, it remains true that the vast majority of children are born as a result of a sexual relationship between a man and a woman, and the Legislature could find that this will continue to be true. The Legislature could also find that such relationships are all too often casual or temporary. It could find that an important function of marriage is to create more stability and permanence in the relationships that cause children to be born. It thus could choose to offer an inducement—in the form of marriage and its attendant benefits—to opposite-sex couples who make a solemn, long-term commitment to each other.[42]

The second reason the court offers for the legislature's rationale has to do with children's socialization into proper gender roles: "The Legislature could rationally believe that it is better, other things being equal, for children to grow up with both a mother and a father. Intuition and experience suggest that a child benefits from having before his or her eyes, every day, living models of what a man and a woman are like." These arguments, clearly intended to project rationality into the legislative mind, rely on the same logical strategies as *Standhardt* and *Morrison*. Although the court purports to be concerned with the "welfare of children" (a point reiterated at least thrice throughout the opinion), clearly the intended beneficiaries of marriage are only the children of heterosexual couples, a point noted by Judge Kaye in dissent. Moreover, as Judge Kaye observes, "Marriage is about much more than producing children, yet same-sex couples are excluded from the entire spectrum of protections that come with civil marriage—purportedly to encourage other people to procreate."[43]

As the procreation argument continued to develop during this period, additional aspects of its inner workings began to appear. In *Conway v. Deane* (2007), the Maryland Court of Appeals heard a case initiated by nine lesbian and gay couples and one individual gay male challenging Maryland's refusal to grant them marriage licenses. In a lengthy, detailed, and careful opinion, the court majority denied their claims, arguing, in large part, that distinctions based on sexual orientation were not subject to heightened scrutiny, that lesbian and gay marriage was not a fundamental right, and that the Maryland Equal Rights Amendment—

prohibiting discrimination on the basis of sex—was inapplicable in the case of lesbian and gay marriage.

As in the cases described earlier, the *Conway* court engages the procreation argument at length, but in that opinion readers also get a glimpse of an additional element. Referencing an earlier case involving child custody, the court found that the Maryland Equal Rights Amendment prohibited sex discrimination between men and women as classes, not as individuals. But en route to that destination the court summarized the earlier decision as follows:

> In that case, James M. Giffin and Donna L. Crane entered, upon their divorce, an agreement whereby Mr. Giffin was awarded physical custody of the couple's two daughters. The agreement provided for annual reviews by a disinterested mental health professional, at the request of the non-custodial parent, of the residential status of the children. Ms. Crane requested in 1995 an annual review of the residential status of the children and, following an unfavorable recommendation by the health professional, filed in the Circuit Court for Montgomery County a petition for modification of custody. The trial court granted the petition, holding that, even though both parents were otherwise qualified to care for the children, the daughters' particular need for a female influence was a "necessary factor" in the court's determination that the mother should be granted custody.[44]

Although the Maryland court makes little of this gender socialization argument for the purposes at hand, it is an aspect of the procreation argument that began to appear in more elaborate form as the debate continued.

In 2008 the Connecticut Supreme Court joined what was, at that time, a small number of courts to rule in favor of marriage rights for lesbian and gay couples. In that case, *Kerrigan v. Commissioner of Public Health*, the majority held that the state's law limiting marriage to straight couples was a violation of the state's constitution. The majority opinion is detailed, carefully explaining that the statute discriminated on the basis of gender and that it therefore should be subjected to heightened scrutiny. Although each of the three dissenting opinions takes issue with the majority's equal protection and due process analyses, Justice Zarella's dissent introduces some additional informative points.

After faulting the majority for failing to address, "during the entire course of its 129 page opinion," to identify, or to discuss "the actual *purpose* of marriage laws" (emphasis in original), Justice Zarella asserts that that purpose is to "privilege and regulate procreative conduct," and thus gay and lesbian persons who "wish to enter into a same sex marriage are not similarly situated to persons who wish to enter into a traditional marriage." Justice Zarella also subscribes to the view that marriage is a timeless, unchanging, and essentialist institution: "The ancient definition of marriage as the union of one man and one woman has its basis in biology, not bigotry." Elsewhere in the opinion he writes "that one man should be joined to one woman in a constant society of cohabiting together . . . is necessary for the propagation of the species, and for the preservation and education of their offspring." At first glance, the procreation argument operates in Justice Zarella's opinion much as it does elsewhere. Marriage, he writes, is about honoring and privileging the only type of relationship that can result in the birth of a child. But his essentialist perspective contains other elements. In order to ensure that "society is not unduly burdened by irresponsible procreation, marriage imposes obligations on the couple to care for each other and for any resulting children." But this view of heterosexual irresponsibility goes further than simply biology: "As I discuss more fully in the text of this opinion, the majority's belief that the ability of a couple to conceive children is an insignificant distinction in the marriage context simply begs the central question in this case by *assuming* that the essence of marriage is a loving and committed relationship. That assumption is unfounded." Although Justice Zarella does not push the point, the assumption that marriage is about the emotional fulfillment of the partners involved often surfaced in the debate as a way to dismiss the claims of lesbian and gay plaintiffs. In its fullest form, the argument was usually used to support the claim that lesbian and gay couples are selfish, disregard the needs of their children, and think only of their own happiness. Historical evidence is of little use to Justice Zarella. He observes, in a footnote, that lesbian and gay marriage existed in ancient times, among Roman emperors, but as he puts it, "Rome's degenerate aristocracy in which murder was rampant and even a horse could be made a senator" was something we would reject today. Also, like many others, Justice Zarella pushes the procreation argument down a slippery slope with worries about polygamy and again reiterates that there is "no deeply rooted history, tradition or practice of same sex marriage, or of marriage defined as a loving, committed relationship, in this nation or in this state."[45]

In addition to chaotic procreation and slippery slides into degeneracy, Justice Zarella elaborates on the need to preserve straight marriage in the interests of gender socialization. Explaining why the state could choose to privilege straight marriage, he writes that "the state rationally could conclude that children do best when they are raised by a mother and a father, a belief that finds great support in life experience and common sense." Citing an article by Katherine Young and Paul Nathanson, Zarella offers readers the following in a footnote: "Boys cannot learn how to become healthy men from even the most loving mother (or pair of mothers) alone. And girls cannot learn how to become healthy women from even the most loving father (or pair of fathers) alone." Gender alone, however, is not what Justice Zarella believes must be taught: "Because heterosexuality is directly related to both reproduction and survival [of the species], and because it involves much more than copulation, every human society has had to promote it actively (although some have also allowed homosexuality in specific circumstances). And marriage is the major way of doing so."[46] Perhaps more surprisingly, he sides with the postmodernists in claiming that heterosexuality, and by implication gender, must be modeled, performed, and socially reinforced in order to be sustained. Where he differs from them, however, is in the belief that society can survive without them.

Donaldson v. State of Montana (2012) began when several lesbian and gay couples sued the state because they were unable to obtain the protections and benefits available to married, different-sex couples. They did not challenge the state's ban on lesbian and gay marriage but instead asked for an injunction prohibiting the state from denying them access to those protections and benefits. The court's majority opinion is short, characterizing the plaintiffs' request as overly broad and beyond the scope of the judiciary. The court does, however, remand the case to the lower court and grants the plaintiffs an opportunity to amend their complaint in order to specify which statute or statutes are at issue and on what legal grounds they are challenging their exclusion from them. A detailed concurring opinion, filed by Justice Rice, takes the procreation argument to extremity.

Early in his opinion Justice Rice informs readers that "marriage between a man and a woman is a unique relationship, dissimilar to all other relationships and alone essential to the nation's foundation and survival, and the State errs neither by recognizing it as such nor by giving it exclusive treatment. In sum, it is not discrimination to treat uniquely that which is unique."[47] After noting that the fundamental right to marriage is so well established that he "need not belabor the point," Judge Rice cites extensively from past cases about the importance of marriage, most notably regarding the relationship between marriage, citizenship, and the state: marriage is "the first step from barbarism to incipient civilization, the purest tie of social life and the true basis of human progress." Borrowing from *Conway v. Deane*, he strikes the biological note and explains that marriage is inextricably bound up with procreation, "which necessarily and biologically involves participation (in ways either intimate or remote) by a man and a woman." Echoing the postmodernist perspective referenced by Justice Zarella, he also depicts heterosexuality as an institution that must be performed and modeled for each generation: "Married couples role-model and thereby teach procreative relationships and the procreative lifestyle to children of the marriage as they are raised, ensuring that marriage's human race-sustaining functions upon which the survival and stability of society depend are passed to and replicated by the next generation."[48] So, for Justice Rice, socialization of children into a heterosexual norm is a key aspect of what marriage does. But, there is more to it than that:

> The replication, by children, of the procreative marital relationship as role-modeled by their married parents not only perpetuates the race-sustaining function by populating the race, but also builds extended families which share hereditary characteristics of a common gene pool. Throughout history, this genetic commonality has provided an invaluable tool to enhance human survival. Common hereditary traits provide critical understanding of an extended family's physical and mental strengths, weaknesses, and susceptibility to disease and death. Even before the advent of modern science, this information was collectively shared among extended family members and served to alert and prepare them for eventualities related to the onset

> of disease and other life patterns, thus strengthening their health and livelihood. Modern medical technologies have only increased this capability, as research of an extended family's genetics now serves to predict, detect, and treat common, family-related diseases, further enhancing human survival. Upon extended families are built people groups or ethnic groups of individual races, tribes, kindred, and nationalities based upon their broadly shared genetic characteristics.[49]

Here we see the procreation argument being enlisted to serve even more essentialist purposes. In addition to heterosexual marriage providing an ideal setting for the gender socialization of children, it is also in society's best interests for the genetic links between people to remain unclouded by assisted reproductive technologies or adoption. This level of rhetorical detail linking marriage, procreation, and survival of the species is unusual. Yet Justice Rice continues:

> When asked during oral argument what unique legal concreteness would remain to marriage if the requested relief was granted, Plaintiffs' counsel replied, "How people view it, how symbolic and how important and how solemn it is, is important. Marriage is meaningful." When asked again, "In what way? I'm trying to understand what concrete[ness] in the law is left?" Counsel responded, "The significance is that you're married." However such a diminished concept of marriage would necessitate a dramatic rewriting of the law. Marriage has always been much more—a concrete legal status which the law recognized and favored with exclusive treatment, including benefits and obligations.[50]

It seems that for Justice Rice straight marriage must be maintained not only because of its role-modeling necessity but also because extending marriage rights to lesbian and gay couples would diminish the institution by taking procreation and heterosexual role-modeling out of the equation. Marriage, if reduced to its symbolic value, is, on this reading, of little value.

Justice Rice also finds other virtues in the institution of marriage:

> [S]o far as heterosexuals are concerned, the evidence that on average married couples live longer, are healthier, earn more, have lower rates of

> substance abuse and mental illness, are less likely to commit suicide, and report higher levels of happiness—that marriage civilizes young males, confers economies of scale and of joint consumption, minimizes sexually transmitted disease, and provides a stable and nourishing framework for child rearing—refutes any claim that policies designed to promote marriage are irrational.[51]

Why gays and lesbians should not be allowed to enjoy such benefits is never explained, but the most important part of this passage is the set of brackets around the initial "s" with which it begins. Cited to *Irizarry v. Bd. of Educ. of Chicago*, and an opinion written by Judge Richard Posner, this passage is taken out of context. In *Irizarry* the plaintiff sued the Chicago Board of Education, alleging that its policy of extending domestic partner benefits only to lesbian and gay couples, and not straight ones, discriminated against unmarried straight couples. Judge Posner's opinion makes a hash of the argument, affirms the lower court's dismissal of the case, and offers some unexpected insights into his thoughts on homosexuality and marriage. The school board proffered two reasons for its policy: (1) to offer to lesbian and gay couples, who could not, at that time, marry, the same benefits that the board offers to straight couples; and (2) to help recruit lesbian and gay teachers who might serve as role models for young gay and lesbian students. Judge Posner's opinion recognizes that the second argument may seem shocking to many, even in 2001, but he clearly supports the board's authority to make such a decision and shows little patience for the plaintiff's claims. Indeed, when asked why, after many years and raising two children, she had not married her partner, Irizarry replied, "[I]t just never came up." Judge Posner's response to this fragment of information underscores his commitment to the institution of marriage: "There may be good reasons why a particular couple would not marry even after producing children, but that the thought of marriage would not even occur to them is disquieting." Judge Rice's quote in *Donaldson* has precisely the opposite effect as that intended by Judge Posner. Judge Posner's, clearly intended to extol the virtues of marriage, not only recognizes the national policy in favor of marriage over cohabitation but also is designed to recognize that while gays and lesbians were excluded from marriage, Irizarry and her partner neglected to avail themselves of an opportunity from which they could have benefited. Moreover, prior to the bracketed "S," Judge Posner wrote, "True, it is no longer widely popular to try to pressure homosexuals to marry persons of the opposite sex. But . . . ," and here is where the bracketed "S" enters the passage. The paragraph concludes with Judge Posner noting that a policy favoring marriage for those who might marry is distinct from a policy offering benefits to couples who cannot. Moreover, the citations that Judge Rice omitted from Judge Posner's opinion reference antigay zealots such as Maggie Gallagher, David Popenoe, and George Dent. Taken in its entirety, Judge Posner's opinion shows a gloss of impatience with the plaintiff's argument as well as an almost snide belittling of its antigay implications. Judge Rice's quote, taken out of context, is used for a very different purpose, that is, to prop up the importance and sanctity of straight marriage as an institution that is threatened and diminished by the potential of expansion to lesbian and gay couples.

In *Jackson v. Abercrombie* (2012), a U.S. District Court in Hawaii rejected the claims of lesbian and gay plaintiffs. Although that ruling was subsequently vacated and remanded as moot, that opinion also invokes the argument for gender socialization:

> The legislature could also rationally conclude that other things being equal, it is best for children to be raised by a parent of each sex. Under rational basis review, as long as the rationale for a classification is at least debatable, the classification is constitutional. Both sides presented evidence on this issue and both sides pointed out flaws in their opponents' evidence. Thus, the Court concludes this rationale is at least debatable and therefore sufficient.[52]

Although the gender socialization argument is presented here as "at least debatable," it is noteworthy as a continuing expansion of the ways the procreation argument became more elaborate and detailed as the debate continued.

Deconstitutive Elaborations

In the marriage debate, such opinions were crafted to uphold the marriage ban with recourse to a particular narrative, one that queer literary scholar Lee Edelman calls “reproductive futurism.” On Edelman’s reading, marriage is among the schematic resources by which a heterosexual ideology symbolizes more than just a particular type of sexual act. Indeed, in this narrative the act of sex is eclipsed, and the associated identity category is infused with a much larger meaning. The usual arrangement of these terms associates homosexuality with excessive desire and carnality while removing gay and lesbian people from the definition of family. Meanwhile, heterosexuality is elevated above this nastiness to stand for the possibility of the future itself; the future of the family, nation, civilization, and the species are all hinged on its (desexualized) implications.[53]

The textual evidence presented in this chapter demonstrates that procreation and child rearing were, for a time, no longer a single, seamless, construct in the marital schema. They were linked when necessary to sustain heterosexual marriage but were separated to exclude lesbian and gay couples from recognition. At the same time that U.S. courts refused to recognize lesbian and gay relationships, they were, with increasing frequency, enforcing the parental obligations of gay and lesbian parents. Despite the volatility of the marriage debate in many states, courts regularly enforced the parental obligations of adoptive co-parents, further attesting to the fact that marriage and child rearing were being distinguished legally.[54] Thus, the heterosexual/marriage/procreation triumvirate became more complex, and it is the latter term that was being redefined in the service of maintaining the other two. Logically, the procreation argument cannot refer primarily to child rearing if it is to allow marriages between nonprocreative straight couples while enforcing the parental obligations of gays and lesbians whose relationships the state refuses to sanction. Splitting the constitutionally protected right to straight marriage from the other possibility of civil unions or domestic partnerships began a process of rhetorically distancing gays and lesbians from straights, but the legal bifurcation of those two rights claims could not succeed for long. Sustaining that bifurcation required evidence, and as is often the case in legal discourse, science was enlisted to that end. Here, the biological realities of human reproduction were being conscripted to serve this purportedly objective, scientific, evidentiary purpose. If procreation was to remain schematically linked to the well-being of children, either it must pertain to both groups, or lesbian and gay couples must be kept from becoming parents.[55] Excluding the children of lesbian and gay couples from the protections of marriage while enforcing those protections through adoption negated the possibility that the procreation argument was about children. As Judge Reichler stated in an opinion dismissing the criminal prosecution of two Unitarian Universalist ministers after they solemnized the unions of lesbian and gay couples in New York: "Citing 'procreation' as a broad justification for denying marriage to same-sex couples displays an anti-gay bias, rather than a real desire to provide a favorable environment for procreation and child-rearing. If family and children were the priority, the state would take all possible steps to protect them."[56] In order for these arguments to remain logical, we must recognize that they signify something else. Closer inspection of the texts cited here and the evidence upon which those arguments are built indicates that that something else is sex.

The narrative of reproductive futurism was at stake in this debate. Citations taken from the U.S. Supreme Court assure us that marriage is an essential component of civilization, without which the species would cease to exist. The argument is made more specific in *Wilson*, where readers find that marriage provides for the orderly continuance of the United States. As the *Singer* court stated, heterosexuals do not even need to have sex. and as *Morrison* reminds us, all it takes is one instance of intercourse for a straight couple to produce a child. These claims fit within the narrative of reproductive futurism by desexualizing heterosexuality while reinforcing its crucial role in making the future (of everything) possible. But because the procreative argument can no longer be logically linked specifically to child rearing in order to exclude lesbian and gay couples, the narrative narrowed and reversed course. Rather than looking forward and seeing procreation as child rearing, the oppositionists looked backward, rendering marriage as a way for the state to regulate the "unintended" consequences of heterosexual sex. Marriage "ameliorates" the problem of children who "arrive unexpectedly," whether their parents planned to have them or not, and provides regularity to what various writers predict would otherwise be "chaotic." Rather than expand the definition of procreation to look forward and include adoption or assisted reproductive technologies, these rhetorical strategies signify what might be called domain constriction.[57] *Procreation*, contrary to the concurrence's opinion in *Lewis*, is no longer operating in the public realm where marriage matters. What is being regulated, ostensibly in the interests of the family and child rearing, nation, and civilization, is copulation—a purely private behavior—an interpretation that divorces procreation from marriage in a way that allows us to see the former as part of an ongoing, lifelong process. These scripts shift our attention to how that process begins—the moment of conception. Furthermore, to draw again from *Morrison*, because lesbian and gay couples do not need marriage in order to demonstrate an intention to become parents and provide a stable home for children, they are placed not only outside the law but above it. Working strenuously to sustain this narrative is not just disingenuous; it is damaging. As Edelman points out, worrying about the rights of some symbolic, figural child may sustain the cultural superiority of heterosexuality, but at the expense of limiting rights and benefits afforded to "real" citizens, "real" children.[58] The ironies, inconsistencies, and logical gaps of the procreation argument were not lost on everyone, however. The following chapter shows how other judges recognized, and compensated for, these lapses in reason.

3

Children by the Carload

Case opinions considered in the previous chapter show how the procreation argument was marshaled in opposition to lesbian and gay marriage and, ultimately, how it developed and became more elaborate. In those opinions the argument was asserted, with much success, in a manner that was dispositive; lesbian and gay couples cannot reproduce "naturally" and thus do not need marriage. Case opinions examined in this chapter show that as the argument was advanced more forcefully and engaged seriously by judges, it began to collapse under its own illogical weight. The rhetorical development of the argument by those opposed to lesbian and gay marriage had deconstitutive tendencies that shone a spotlight on the messiness and disorder of heterosexuality, marriage, and reproduction while extolling the virtues of deliberate family formation by lesbian and gay couples. These opinions, penned by judges who favored marriage rights for lesbian and gay couples, suggest a different narrative arc. Here, in the early cases, we see that the procreation argument appears but is used sparingly. As the debate about marriage rights continued, courts were invited to consider the argument with increasing frequency. Taken seriously at first, and deftly refuted, later cases show that the argument eventually became almost comical.

The story told in this chapter begins with the Hawaii court decisions of 1993. In the years shortly thereafter, many states and the federal government took preemptive measures to ensure that lesbian and gay marriage would be prohibited. The first success of the LGBT movement came from Massachusetts in 2003. Subsequently, efforts spread across the nation, but the focus here is on cases from California, Connecticut, Indiana, Wisconsin, Idaho, and Nevada. While each of the decisions discussed below is part of a larger chain of trials and appeals, these texts illustrate how the conversation changed from one where procreation and marriage could be asserted as a unified concept, to a complex series of interlocking ideas that could also be disassociated from one another. Presented chronologically, these cases show how detailed scrutiny of heterosexuality, the sort characterized as impossible in chapter 1, changed the tone of the legal debate.

Baehr v. Miike (1993)

Baehr v. Miike began when three lesbian and gay couples challenged Hawaii's refusal to grant them marriage licenses. From 1990 to 1999 the case moved between trial and appellate courts, ultimately inspiring legislative intervention and a constitutional amendment in the state. In a decision that set off a national firestorm and inspired passage of the federal Defense of Marriage Act, the Hawaii Supreme Court took a measured approach to the question of marriage rights and did so with little consideration of the procreation argument. The decision foreshadowed the possibility that lesbian and gay marriage may be a new constitutional right. Referring to U.S. Supreme Court decisions regarding the history of marriage, the Hawaii Supreme Court asserted that it was in fact a new right, not a fundamental right protected by the due process clause. Tracing the history of marriage precedents, the Hawaii court found that earlier decisions announcing the sanctity of a right to marriage understood it implicitly as being about straight couples because of the link to procreation. Building on this premise, the court ruled that although the applicant couples did not have a fundamental right to lesbian or gay marriage, they were free to pursue an equal protection claim. In its equal protection analysis the Court asserted that denying marriage rights to lesbian and gay couples was discrimination on the basis of sex. Thus, they remanded the case to a lower court, instructing that court to consider whether or not the state's marriage laws restricting marriage to male-female couples were narrowly tailored to serve a compelling state interest.

Sex and gender are somewhat elided in *Baehr*, yet the court relied on the distinction to support its ruling. Following the intellectual lineage sketched in chapter 1, the court recognized that sex and gender are intertwined but not the same thing; sex, the court recognized, is the biological, physical, aspect of the self situated within a system of meaning called gender, but the court recognized that the terms are separable.[1] Although unarticulated, the distinction allowed the *Baehr* majority to rely on *Holdman v. Olim* (1978) and its link to *Frontiero v. Richardson* (1973) to justify the application of heightened scrutiny. In *Holdman*, the Hawaii court considered whether female visitors to prisons could be required to wear brassieres. In *Frontiero* the U.S. Supreme Court held that married men and women in the military could not be afforded different pay or benefits on the basis of their gender. The *Holdman* court found that penal discipline was a compelling state interest that justified upholding the regulation, but it followed *Frontiero* and ruled that the gendered scheme was unconstitutional. In so doing, the court distinguished between biology (sex and the body) and the social performance of stereotypes associated with that binary system (gender and wearing specific articles of clothing). The distinction is made particularly clear when the *Baehr* court references the attorney general's argument: "Lewin contends that the 'fact that homosexual [*sic*—actually same-sex] partners cannot form a state-licensed marriage is not the product of impermissible discrimination.'" Marriage, the state argued, was a male-female institution throughout history and by definition. The court found this logic to be circular and unpersuasive.[2] Here, the *Baehr* court distinguishes between identity categories (e.g., gay, lesbian, or straight) and biological sex (coitus). By making this move, the court was then capable of advancing an argument built on the distinction. Following *Holdman* and *Frontiero* the court's decision draws the readers' attention to the differences between immutable characteristics and outdated stereotypes associated with them. The bodies of prison visitors, soldiers, and spouses per se are less important; the appropriate realm of analysis is culture—meaning and interpretation. Moving away from sex and toward gender, the court observed, has a universalizing potential because "everyone is gendered, and everyone is negatively affected by the sex-gender system."[3]

Unlike many subsequent opinions, the *Baehr* court paid only passing attention to the procreation argument. The majority took note of the linkage between marriage and procreation when it summarized the Supreme Court's decision in *Skinner v. Oklahoma* (1942). There the Court struck down an Oklahoma statute that provided for the compulsory sterilization of "habitual criminals" and wrote that marriage and procreation were "fundamental to the very existence and survival of the race."[4] Quoting this passage, the *Baehr* court recognized its value and importance yet simultaneously distinguished between that case and the one at hand:

> Whether the court viewed marriage and procreation as a single indivisible right, the least that can be said is that it was obviously contemplating unions between men and women when it ruled that the right to marry was fundamental. This is hardly surprising inasmuch as none of the United States sanctioned any other marriage configuration at the time.[5]

The court repeats the point with respect to the Supreme Court's decision in *Zablocki v. Redhail* (1978), which struck down a Wisconsin statute that prevented people from marrying if they were in arrears on their child support obligations. Noting that the court in *Zablocki* implicitly recognized only marriages between men and women, the *Baehr* court observed: "Once again, this is hardly surprising inasmuch as such unions are the only state-sanctioned marriages currently acknowledged in this country."[6] Having set aside the necessity of linking marriage and procreation, the *Baehr* court then reframed what it saw as the issue at hand:

> [T]he precise question facing this court is whether we will extend the present boundaries of the fundamental right of marriage to include same-sex couples, or, put another way, whether we will hold that same-sex couples possess a fundamental right to marry. In effect, as the applicant couples frankly admit, we are being asked to recognize a new fundamental right.[7]

Whether or not lesbian and gay marriage could be considered a "new" right is a question that returned often throughout the debate, ultimately forming a core argument of Justice Alito's later dissents. The dissenting judge in *Baehr* focused attention on the majority's equal protection analysis as it pertained to gender, leaving aside the procreation argument. Nonetheless, the court's implicit recognition of the difference between sex, construed as biological, essentialist, and procreative, and gender, construed as operating in the domain of culture and meaning, not unlike marriage, foreshadowed cracks that widened as the argument developed. Despite the encouraging signs portended by the *Baehr* decision, it ultimately sparked as much backlash against the movement as it inspired in its favor.[8] Ultimately, however, *Baehr* was instrumental in putting the issue at the center of the LGBT rights agenda.

Goodridge v. Dept. of Public Health (2003)

As noted in chapter 2, Justice Cordy's dissent in the Massachusetts case *Goodridge v. Dept. of Public Health* is regularly cited as the first time the procreation argument appeared in a judicial opinion. Among the reasons Massachusetts offered for its restriction of marriage to straight couples was the claim that such marriages provide "a favorable setting for procreation." The trial court accepted that logic, but the majority of the Massachusetts Supreme Court did not: "This is incorrect. Our laws of civil marriage do not privilege procreative heterosexual intercourse between married people above every other form of adult intimacy and every other means of creating a family."[9] The court summarized the limitations of the procreation argument by observing that neither procreation nor fertility had ever been a prerequisite for marriage; that the exclusive and permanent commitment of marriage partners is the sine qua non of marriage; and that despite the historical links between sex, procreation, and marriage, these constructs are no longer so tightly intertwined:

> [The statute at issue] contains no requirement that the applicants for a marriage license attest to their ability or intention to conceive children by coitus. Fertility is not a condition of marriage, nor is it grounds for divorce. People who have never consummated their marriage, and never plan to, may be and stay married. People who cannot stir from their deathbed may marry. While it is certainly true that many, perhaps most, married couples have children together (assisted or unassisted), it is the exclusive and permanent commitment of the marriage partners to one another, not the begetting of children, that is the sine qua non of civil marriage.[10]

Moreover, the court recognized that the procreation argument "singles out the one unbridgeable difference between same-sex and opposite-sex couples, and transforms that difference into the essence of legal marriage."[11]

The *Goodridge* court emphasized the relationship between partners regardless of their reproductive status or intentions. Additionally, in contrast to Justice Cordy's dissent, the majority focused its attention on the welfare of children and families regardless of how they were conceived:

> Moreover, the Commonwealth affirmatively facilitates bringing children into a family regardless of whether the intended parent is married or unmarried, whether the child is adopted or born into a family, whether assistive technology was used to conceive the child, and whether the parent or her partner is heterosexual, homosexual, or bisexual. If procreation were a necessary component of civil marriage, our statutes would draw a tighter circle around the permissible bounds of nonmarital child bearing and the creation of families by noncoital means. The attempt to isolate procreation as "the source of a fundamental right to marry" overlooks the integrated way in which courts have examined the complex and overlapping realms of personal autonomy, marriage, family life, and child rearing. Our jurisprudence recognizes that, in these nuanced and fundamentally private areas of life, such a narrow focus is inappropriate.[12]

Here the Court parses the procreation argument into its constitutive elements—marital status, methods of reproduction, sexual orientation—and rejects the assertion that they must be understood as a unified whole. Indeed, as the Court observes, the state strives to protect the welfare of children regardless of their parents' marital status, sexual orientation, or the methods by which couples become parents: "Protecting the welfare of children is a paramount State policy. Restricting marriage to opposite-sex couples, however, cannot plausibly further this policy." The court also recognized that lesbians and gays constituted a "sizeable class of parents" who were being denied the protections of marriage: "It cannot be rational under our laws, and indeed it is not permitted, to penalize children by depriving them of State benefits because the State disapproves of their parents' sexual orientation."[13]

The Court also considered the state's purported interest in preserving resources but was not persuaded by that line of argument:

> The department suggests additional rationales for prohibiting same-sex couples from marrying, which are developed by some amici. It argues that broadening civil marriage to include same-sex couples will trivialize or destroy the institution of marriage as it has historically been fashioned. Certainly our decision today marks a significant change in the definition of marriage as it has been inherited from the common law, and understood by many societies for centuries. But it does not disturb the funda-

> mental value of marriage in our society. Here, the plaintiffs seek only to be married, not to undermine the institution of civil marriage. They do not want marriage abolished.[14]

The Court detailed the myriad changes that marriage has undergone throughout history—the move toward no-fault divorce, the inclusion of interracial couples, expansion of the rights of married women—and observed that the institution remains vibrant in the face of such changes. One of the arguments put forward most forcefully by the majority in *Goodridge* was that marriage is in the best interests of children, regardless of how those children came into their families and regardless of the sexual orientation of the parents. The Court has no doubt that marriage as an institution will survive the expansion to include lesbian and gay couples, too: "If anything, extending civil marriage to same-sex couples reinforces the importance of marriage to individuals and communities."[15] Setting aside the unbridgeable gap between sex, gender, and procreation, the *Goodridge* court followed the lead that began with *Baehr* by turning away from the moment of conception and focusing attention instead on children.

In re Marriage Cases (2006)

This cluster of consolidated cases started in 2004 when city officials in San Francisco began issuing marriage licenses to same-sex couples. What resulted was one of the longest-running, most complicated series of cases in the marriage debate, moving from trial courts to appellate courts, to the California Supreme Court, and through the California referendum process in the form of Proposition 8. In October 2006 the California Court of Appeals reviewed a lower court ruling from San Francisco that overturned California's statutes defining marriage as between only a man and a woman. One of the important things to notice about *In re Marriage Cases* is that the state's attorney general disavowed the procreation argument when presenting the case. Nevertheless, the majority opinion invoked it anyway, linking marriage to biological reproduction of "unintended offspring" and noting that prior to the advent of reproductive technologies, "only heterosexual couples were capable of procreating."[16]

As with many of the opinions in support of lesbian and gay marriage, Judge Kline's dissent engages with the procreation argument interpreted through the lenses of *Loving*, *Zablocki*, and *Turner*. In short, his objective is to refute the assertion that a right to lesbian and gay marriage is a very new right as the *Baehr* court had indicated and, instead, to establish that marriage is a long-recognized fundamental right that should apply equally to all couples regardless of sexual orientation. His opening paragraph encapsulates the point by asserting that the present case was no more about a right to lesbian and gay marriage than *Loving* was about a right to interracial marriage, or that *Bowers* was about the right of homosexuals to engage in sodomy. Judge Kline also observes that the state's attorney general refused to advance the procreation argument because the state of California recognizes the importance of protecting children, including those of gays and lesbians, and that developing the procreation argument would have been contrary to the state's official policy. Moreover, in his summary critique of the majority opinion and the authorities it cites, Judge Kline argues that under their proposed interpretation, "marriage is not defined by love and commitment, by the benefits it confers and the burdens it entails, or even by children, but rather by its exclusion of homosexuals—that is, by its discriminatory aspect."[17]

One of the more novel and insightful aspects of Judge Kline's dissent is the way he roots the procreation argument in religious doctrine. He summarizes multiple different approaches taken by other courts to deny marriage rights to lesbian and gay couples, including their reliance on dictionaries for definitions of marriage, the procreation argument, and its link to the survival of the species. Although such arguments are disavowed by the court majority, he notes that they were presented by several amici, and thus he addresses them directly. More insightfully, he observes that although courts could not openly rely on religious objections to lesbian and gay marriage, finding that religion provides the "subtext of some opinions that do not dwell on the subject."[18] Borrowing from the text of another court's opinion, Judge Kline proposes that the argument linking marriage to religious doctrine operates as follows: marriage is governed by civil law; civil law is rooted in English civil law; English civil law took its basic principles from canon law; canon law emerged from ecclesiastical courts; canon law in Judaism and Christianity could not possibly sanction lesbian and gay marriage because of vehement condemnation of homosexuality in scripture; same-sex marriage is thus "*unthinkable and, by definition, impossible*."[19] In order to disrupt this circular chain of logic, Judge Kline proceeds to demonstrate how Supreme Court precedents explicitly refuted the link between marriage and procreation. He begins with *Griswold*:

> *Griswold* makes no reference to procreation; and the precise holding of *Griswold*, that the state could not criminalize a married couple's use of contraceptives, is itself incompatible with the proposition that the constitutionally protected status of marriage turns on its relationship to procreation.[20]

Similarly, Judge Kline observes, because *Turner* involved inmates who, in many instances, would never be able to consummate their marriages, it could not stand for the proposition that marriage and procreation were inextricably linked. He also asserts, like many others, that the responsible procreation argument's outcome of excluding the children of gay and lesbian couples from the protections of marriage does nothing to further the interests of children who are "accidentally conceived."[21] During the thirteen years between *Baehr* and the California marriage cases, litigants increasingly pressed their claims in court, asking for the right to marry. Heterosexuality was being put on trial.

Kerrigan v. Commissioner of Public Health (2008)

In *Kerrigan v. Commissioner of Public Health*, the Supreme Court of Connecticut ruled in favor of lesbian and gay plaintiffs, arguing that the state's statutory scheme prohibiting their marriages ran afoul of both the due process clause and the equal protection clause of the state constitution. Like the Massachusetts court in *Goodridge*, the Connecticut Supreme Court engaged the procreation argument briefly, primarily in response to the dissent; but, unlike the Massachusetts court, the Connecticut court was also invited to address the fact that that state had enacted a civil union statute that gave all the legal benefits of marriage to lesbian and gay couples. Early in the opinion the Connecticut court referenced the U.S. Supreme Court's jurisprudence on marriage (i.e., it is a fundamental right; the basis of civilization; the foundation of family, nation, and history), and those citations were presented without reference to the procreation argument. But, as the court noted:

> In his dissent, Justice Zarella alone asserts that same sex and opposite sex couples who wish to marry are not similarly situated because the former cannot engage in procreative sexual conduct. In view of the myriad and important similarities between same sex and opposite sex couples, including their shared interest in having and raising a family, we disagree that the inability of the former to conceive children together defeats the plaintiffs' equal protection challenge. Although it may be argued that the state's interest in regulating procreative conduct constitutes a rational basis for limiting marriage to opposite sex couples—an argument that, notably, the state itself expressly has disavowed—that rationale does not answer the entirely different question of whether same sex and opposite sex couples are similarly situated for present purposes. Because same sex and opposite sex couples have the same interest in having a family and the same right to do so, the mere fact that children of the former may be conceived in a different manner than children of the latter is insufficient, standing alone, to negate the fundamental and overriding similarities that they share, both with regard to matters relating to family and in all other respects. Thus, even though procreative conduct plays an important role in many marriages, we do not believe that such conduct so defines the institution of marriage that the inability to engage in that conduct is determinative of whether same sex and opposite sex couples are similarly situated for equal protection purposes, especially in view of the fact that some opposite sex couples also are unable to procreate, and others choose not to do so.[22]

Although the majority opinion references procreation, procreative conduct, and the ability to procreate, it does so in order to refute the arguments in dissent. The first reference not addressed to the dissent cites a passage from *Casey* as it was used in *Lawrence* to uphold the rights of gay people to define their intimate lives as they deem appropriate. The second reference arrives in a passage wherein the majority explains that the state had specifically disavowed the argument that prohibiting same-sex marriage could steer more heterosexuals into procreative relationships.

The more pressing concern for the Connecticut court was the distinction between marriage and civil unions. Referring to the trial court's decision in that case, the Connecticut Supreme Court concluded that the lower court improperly "determined that the distinction between civil unions and marriage is constitutionally insignificant merely because a same sex couple who enters into a civil union enjoys the same legal rights as an opposite sex couple who enters into a marriage." Moreover, the court concluded that the statutory scheme establishing two separate (but ostensibly equal) institutions discriminated against lesbian and gay people on the basis of their sexual orientation.[23]

One of the more persuasive arguments put forward by the majority in this opinion was that separate institutions, that is, marriage for heterosexuals and civil unions for gays and lesbians, violated equal protection. In this case the lower court held that gays and lesbians were not subjected to discrimination because the legislature had provided them with access to civil unions. This inspired the Connecticut Supreme Court to elaborate on the meaning and value of marriage:

> The plaintiffs challenge the trial court's conclusion that the distinction between marriage and civil unions is merely one of nomenclature. They contend that marriage is not simply a term denominating a bundle of legal rights. Rather, they contend that it is an institution of unique and enduring importance in our society, one that carries with it a special status.[24]

The court continues:

> Indeed, marriage has been characterized as "intimate to the degree of being sacred"; and "an institution more basic in our civilization than any other." Marriage, therefore, is not merely shorthand for a discrete set of legal rights and responsibilities but is "one of the most fundamental of human relationships. . . ." "Marriage . . . bestows enormous private and social advantages on those who choose to marry. Civil marriage is at once a deeply personal commitment to another human being and a highly public celebration of the ideals of mutuality, companionship, intimacy, fidelity, and family. . . . Because it fulfills yearnings for security, safe haven, and connection that express our common humanity, civil marriage is an esteemed institution."[25]

One of the notable aspects of this passage is that it is used to demonstrate the importance of marriage, and it does so without referencing procreation. Recognizing the "exalted status" of marriage in our society, the court asserted that it was "hardly surprising" that civil unions would be perceived as inferior to marriage: "Maintaining a second-class citizen status for same-sex couples by excluding them from the institution of civil marriage *is* the constitutional infirmity at issue."[26] Having brought all the elements of marriage as an institution together, the court refuses to take them apart. In a footnote the court explains:

> We agree with the following point made by the Lambda Legal Defense and Education Fund, Inc., in its amicus brief: "Any married couple [reasonably] would feel that they had lost something precious and irreplaceable if the government were to tell them that they no longer were 'married' and instead were in a 'civil union.' The sense of being 'married'—what this conveys to a couple and their community, and the security of having others clearly understand the fact of their marriage and all it signifies—would be taken from them. These losses are part of what same sex couples are denied when government assigns them a 'civil union' status. If the tables were turned, very few heterosexuals would countenance being told that they could enter only civil unions and that marriage is reserved for lesbian and gay couples. Surely there is [a] constitutional injury when the majority imposes on the minority that which it would not accept for itself.

Marriage, on the court's reading, is a sacred institution with a deep history of meaning and significance. But even more important, the court recognizes that while it is a "union that sanctifies sex," others take a different view, one that confirms "the most profound possible commitment."[27] These meanings, the court noted, attached to the institution after centuries of experience. Civil unions, in contrast, could not approximate its meaning and value. In these passages the court weaves lesbian and gay couples into the institution of marriage and confers upon them the dignity and social status associated with it.

In a challenge to the logic put forward by Justice Borden in dissent, the court majority highlighted the inconsistency inherent in asserting that marriage and civil unions were of equal value and meaning. The passage merits quoting in full:

We are confused by the position that Justice Borden takes in his dissenting opinion with respect to the plaintiffs' contention that they have alleged a cognizable constitutional claim. Justice Borden first expresses the view that the plaintiffs have set forth a claim sufficient to "trigger equal protection analysis" because of the "uncertainty" as to whether civil unions "now or soon will be viewed by the citizens of our state as the social equivalent of marriage." Before engaging in this analysis, however, Justice Borden states that "our experience with civil unions is simply too new and the views of the people of our state about it as a social institution are too much in flux to say with any certitude that the marriage statute must be struck down in order to vindicate the plaintiffs' constitutional rights." This latter assertion is inconsistent with Justice Borden's earlier acknowledgment that, contrary to the decision of the trial court, the plaintiffs have set forth a claim that implicates the equal protection provisions of the state constitution.

Nevertheless, with respect to Justice Borden's assertion that the plaintiffs have failed to demonstrate, to any reasonable degree of certainty, that the institution of marriage enjoys a greater status in our society than civil unions, for the reasons set forth by the trial court, we question whether, under that view, the plaintiffs have satisfied their burden of demonstrating actual harm. Moreover, Justice Borden's contention that there is insufficient reason to conclude that civil unions are not viewed as the "social equivalent" of marriage cannot be reconciled with his own acknowledgment that, in stark contrast to civil unions, marriage "is a fundamental and ancient social institution that has existed in our state from before its founding and throughout the world for millennia." We do not see how the recently created legal entity of civil union possibly can embody the same status as an institution of such long-standing and overriding societal importance as marriage. If proof of this obvious fact were necessary, it would suffice to point out that the vast majority of heterosexual couples would be unwilling to give up their constitutionally protected right to marry in exchange for the bundle of legal rights that the legislature has denominated a civil union. In addition, Justice Borden's assertion that the issue is irretrievably fact-bound and, therefore, falls outside this court's authority, is surprising in view of his willingness to marshal evidence from hearsay sources not in the record of this case and to draw conclusive inferences from those sources with respect to the

> relative political power of gay persons. In sum, Justice Borden's refusal to concede the obvious hardly reflects the wisdom to which Judge Learned Hand was referring when he reminded us that judges should never be too certain that they are right; rather, it brings to mind the admonition of former United States Supreme Court Justice Felix Frankfurter that we "should not be ignorant as judges of what we know as men [and women]."[28]

With this forceful rebuttal to the arguments made in dissent, the Connecticut court exposed the lapses in logic put forward by proponents of the procreation argument. Moreover, the court was determined to make clear that civil unions, however beneficial they may be, lacked the deep historical, cultural meaning attributable to marriage. Echoing Judge Kline, quoted earlier, the Connecticut court refused to define marriage by its exclusion of homosexuals. In addition, the court rejected the state's argument that lesbian/gay and straight couples are not similarly situated for the purposes of equal protection analysis. In the text of the opinion the court notes that both types of couples seek to enter into committed, loving relationships where they can raise their children in a stable environment. At the same time that heterosexuality was being put on trial, attempts to institutionalize civil unions as "separate but equal" were failing to persuade a more enlightened audience.

Baskin v. Bogan (2014)

In *Baskin v. Bogan*, lesbian and gay couples successfully challenged the marriage prohibition statutes in Indiana and Wisconsin. They were successful at the district court level, and by the time Judge Posner for the Seventh Circuit Court of Appeals penned his opinion in the case, lesbian and gay marriages were being recognized in nineteen states.

Judge Posner's opinion—one that might be described as impatient, incredulous, sarcastic, wry, and possibly even comical—must be classified as among the most child-centric as well as one of the most essentialist opinions issued on the subject. His impatience with the states' arguments becomes apparent immediately at the outset. After summarizing the procedural history of the case in a spare two-sentence paragraph, Judge Posner's third and fourth sentences set the stage for what was to come: "Formally these cases are about discrimination against the small homosexual minority in the United States. But at a deeper level, as we shall see, they are about the welfare of American children."[29] He then proceeds to summarize the procreation argument, characterizing it as the argument the states "press hardest in defense of their prohibition of same-sex marriage" but one that he finds unconvincing. For Judge Posner the central conceit of the argument is that marriage is necessary in order to steer careless heterosexual reproduction into marriages so as to minimize the number of abandoned children. His rejection of this argument is woven throughout the opinion: "Overlooked by this argument is that many of those abandoned children are adopted by homosexual couples, and those children would be better off both emotionally and economically if their adoptive parents were married."[30] The states' argument that lesbian and gay couples don't need marriage because they don't reproduce inadvertently "is so full of holes that it cannot be taken seriously."[31] This rebuttal of the procreation argument returns throughout Judge Posner's opinion but appears most forcefully and amusingly here:

> At oral argument the state's lawyer was asked whether "Indiana's law is about successfully raising children," and since "you agree same-sex couples can successfully raise children, why shouldn't the ban be lifted as to them?" The lawyer answered that "the assumption is that with opposite sex couples there is very little thought given during the sexual act, sometimes, to whether babies may be a consequence." In other words, Indiana's government thinks that straight couples tend to be sexually irresponsible, producing unwanted children by the carload, and so must be pressured (in the form of governmental encouragement of marriage through a combination of sticks and carrots) to marry, but that gay couples, unable as they are to produce children wanted or unwanted, are model parents—model citizens really—so have no need for marriage. Heterosexuals get drunk and pregnant, producing unwanted children; their reward is to be allowed to marry. Homosexual couples do not produce unwanted children; their reward is to be denied the right to marry. Go figure.[32]

Judge Posner's impatience is obvious. It also merits note that he resisted such a dour and careless understanding of heterosexuality, and his resistance took a scientific albeit essentialist form. His opinion drew on social science evidence to claim that homosexuals make up between 1.5 percent and 4 percent of the population;[33] he cited research suggesting that causes of homosexuality are either genetic or neurobiological.[34] He also asserted that these biological factors may have a larger social and evolutionary purpose:

> Although it seems paradoxical to suggest that homosexuality could have a genetic origin, given that homosexual sex is non-procreative, homosexuality may, like menopause, by reducing procreation by some members of society free them to provide child-caring assistance to their procreative relatives, thus increasing the survival and hence procreative aspects of these relatives.[35]

These references to what he calls the "kin selection hypothesis" or the "helper in the nest theory" are not merely refutations of the states' version of the procreation argument; they established a rhetorical foundation for understanding sexual orientation as biologically determined and therefore properly included within a dominant conceptualization of the family.

The opinion is unique in that it attempts to establish a social purpose for homosexuality insofar as it recognizes gays and lesbians not only as members of their own natal families but also as people whose families are beneficial to society as a whole. Moreover, the opinion strives to adjust our understanding of how the children of lesbians and gays fit into a larger social framework:

> Consider now the emotional comfort that having married parents is likely to provide to children adopted by same-sex couples. Suppose such a child comes home from school one day and reports to his parents that all his class-mates have a mom and a dad, while he has two moms (or two dads, as the case may be). Children, being natural conformists, tend to be upset upon discovering that they're not in step with their peers. If a child's same-sex parents are married, however, the parents can tell the child truthfully that an adult is permitted to marry a person of the opposite sex, or if the adult prefers as some do a person of his or her own sex, but that either way the parents are married and therefore the child can

> feel secure in being the child of a married couple. Conversely, imagine the parents having to tell their child that same-sex couples can't marry, and so the child is not the child of a married couple, unlike his classmates.[36]

In light of his primary concern with children, as noted at the outset of the opinion, Judge Posner here invites the reader to sympathize with the "naturally conformist" child who, even in childhood, understands the larger meaning and value of marriage. Although the passage skirts another question such a child may ask—Where do babies come from?—setting aside that aspect of the issue drives home what he sees as the value of marriage. Indeed, avoiding this question and its sexualized implications was part of what proponents of the procreation argument hoped to do. But, in furtherance of his point, Judge Posner was unwilling to accept the argument that lesbian and gay marriage in some way destabilizes the centrality of children from marriage and replaces it with the emotional needs of adults. In his consideration of no-fault divorce Judge Posner noted that the state of Wisconsin had argued that "allowing same-sex marriage creates a danger of 'shifting the public understanding of marriage away from a largely child-centric institution to an adult-centric institution focused on emotion.'" This assertion echoes one of the oft-repeated canards about gays and lesbians. It is also a point that returns in Justice Alito's dissents. Judge Posner, however, could find no evidence to support the states' position on the point.[37]

Like many other litigants in this debate, the states' attorneys urged the court to "go slow" in changing their laws. With regard to Indiana's claim on this point, Judge Posner discusses marriages between first and second cousins. Indiana law allows first cousins to marry if the parties are older than sixty-five and thus infertile. Moreover, the state recognizes first- and second-cousin marriages performed in other jurisdictions even without such a showing of age. This discrepancy, one written into the state's legal tradition, signaled to Judge Posner that the state's prohibition on lesbian and gay marriage was not actually about regulating procreation but was instead driven by animus. He underscored the point by reciting a list of other useless traditions such as, Why do men wear ties? Why do people shake hands or kiss each other on the cheek (potentially spreading germs)? Why does the president grant amnesty to turkeys at Thanksgiving? Judge Posner continues:

> [T]hese traditions, while to the fastidious they may seem silly, are at least harmless. If no social benefit is conferred by a tradition and it is written into law and it discriminates against a number of people and does them harm beyond just offending them, it is not just a harmless anachronism; it is a violation of the equal protection clause, as in *Loving*.[38]

He goes on to observe that the state's argument about the "wonders of tradition" overlooks many other marital traditions, namely, polygamy as it is practiced in "Syria, Yemen, Iraq, Iran, Egypt, Sudan, Morocco, and Algeria." Moreover, he observes that polygamy "flourishes in many African countries that do not actually authorize it, as well as in parts of Utah." For emphasis, he then ponders how the "wonders of tradition" bear on the prohibition of lesbian and gay marriage, asking, rhetorically, if the state believes that prohibiting lesbian and gay marriage will somehow channel gay and lesbian people into straight marriages: "Efforts to convert homosexuals to heterosexuality have been a bust; is the opposite conversion more feasible?"[39]

Judge Posner's final assault on the argument from tradition references Justice Alito's dissent from *Windsor*. He cites Justice Alito's observation that we cannot predict with certainty what the long-term ramifications of lesbian and gay marriage will be. Judge Posner countered by observing that it is impossible to know in advance what the long-term effects of *any* constitutional decision might be, but the reality of immediate damage to children caused by the prohibition on lesbian and gay marriage is clear: "The refusal [of Wisconsin to recognize joint adoptions] harms the children by telling them they don't have two parents, like other children, and harms the parent who is not the adoptive parent by depriving him or her of the legal status of a parent. The state offers no justification."[40] He put the final nail in the coffin by characterizing the arguments of Wisconsin and Indiana as being "not only conjectural" but "totally implausible."[41] With Judge Posner's pen, the most garish features of the procreation argument were subjected to thorough scrutiny.

Latta v. Otter (2014)

In *Latta v. Otter*, lesbian and gay couples challenged laws from both Idaho and Nevada that restricted marriage to straight couples and refused to recognize marriages of lesbian and gay couples performed in other states. State officials as well as the activist group Coalition to Protect Marriage argued in response that the laws survived heightened scrutiny because they served the compelling interest of sending the message that "opposite-sex marriage is important because it encourages people who procreate to be responsible parents, and because opposite-sex parents are better for children than same-sex parents."[42] Additionally, the defendants argued that their laws did not discriminate on the basis of sexual orientation but on the basis of procreative capacity. Of the many cases discussed throughout this book, *Latta v. Otter* is one of the most thorough in that the court carefully parses the procreation argument into several different claims and engages with each at length.

The first of the defendants' claims addressed by the court is the assertion that lesbian and gay marriage will lead to an increase in fatherless children. As the court summarizes:

> First, they argue that since same-sex families will not include both a father and a mother, a man who has a child with a woman will conclude that his involvement in that child's life is not essential. They appear to contend that such a father will see a child being raised by two women and deduce that because the state has said it is unnecessary for that child—who has two parents—to have a father, it is also unnecessary for his child to have a father. This proposition reflects a crass and callous view of parental love and the parental bond that is not worthy of response. We reject it out of hand.[43]

This thread of the procreation argument seems to have been intended to invoke social anxieties about single motherhood, but it overlooks as much as it puts forward. The trope of single motherhood, bound up as it is with racialized notions of the nonwhite "welfare queen," is thought to threaten the body politic because such families are depicted as a drain on the public purse. Specifically situating lesbian couples as the symbol of threat, it ignores the message that might be sent by gay male parents and what that might say about motherlessness. There is, however, no corresponding, culturally available trope by which single fathers are seen as an economic liability. While the cases examined in chapter 2 portray heterosexual reproduction as potentially messy and chaotic, the argument being addressed in this passage is a scathing indictment of heterosexual masculinity.

The second thread of the procreation argument addressed by the court considers the possibility that allowing lesbian and gay couples to marry would tarnish the institution of marriage and reduce its value to straight people: "[O]pposite-sex couples who disapprove of same-sex marriage will opt less frequently or enthusiastically to participate in an institution that allows same-sex couples to participate."[44] Here the defendants' argument explicitly accommodates antigay animus in a manner that echoes an argument put forward in Judge Kline's dissent from the California marriage cases discussed earlier. As he noted, many people who object to lesbian and gay marriage do so on religious grounds, but while many religious people hold the sincere belief that homosexuality is morally wrong, all major religions encourage people to marry. It would be nonsensical for religious adherents to ignore the teachings of their own faith or to commit the sin of extramarital sex because they view the actions of others as contrary to scripture. Moreover, to propose that straight couples would avoid marriage because gay couples were allowed it assumes that the value of marriage was already significantly compromised, a diminution of value that could, at the time, only have been caused by straight people. As Judge Kline observed, this particular objection would be sustainable only if the courts accept antigay animus as a valid social norm.

A third thread of argument put forward by the defendants is attenuated to the point of absurdity. Relegated to a footnote, the court wryly dispatches it:

> [Governor Otter] also states, in conclusory fashion, that allowing same-sex marriage will lead opposite-sex couples to abuse alcohol and drugs, engage in extramarital affairs, take on demanding work schedules, and participate in time-consuming hobbies. We seriously doubt that allowing committed same-sex couples to settle down in legally recognized marriages will drive opposite-sex couples to sex, drugs, and rock-and-roll.[45]

The unfathomable chain of causality exposed by the court's treatment of the procreation argument is only one of its startling flaws. Alcoholism, drug abuse, and extramarital affairs may be classifiable as social problems, but demanding work schedules and time-consuming hobbies are not usually lumped in with such company. More damning perhaps are the assumptions it makes about straight people, who, it seems here, are prone to addiction and sexual licentiousness, claims that are more often directed at gay men. The court's wry treatment continues by quoting Judge Posner's quip about straight people producing unwanted children by the carload.

The fourth and most prominent theme of the procreation argument engaged in *Latta v. Otter* considers the meaning of marriage and the family generally, but the focus quickly turns to how those terms are connected to reproduction and what that means for children. Referencing *Lawrence v. Texas* (2003) and the lineage of precedents favoring sexual privacy going back to *Griswold*, Judge Reinhardt writes, "Just as 'it would demean a married couple were it to be said marriage is simply about the right to have sexual intercourse,' it demeans married couples—especially those who are childless—to say that marriage is simply about the capacity to procreate."[46] Inasmuch as marriage has always been a license for sanctioned sexual behavior, speaking that truth is usually seen as devaluing the institution. Here Judge Reinhardt does more than make the compulsory rhetorical move of excising sex from the cultural and symbolic value of marriage; he also locates procreative capacity among those unmentionable taints. Marriage is so much more than simply a license to have sex or to reproduce. But it is not just the institution of marriage that suffers; it is, more important, children who must bear the burden of having parents who are ineligible to marry: "In extending the benefits of marriage only to people who have the capacity to procreate, while denying those same benefits to people who already have children, Idaho and Nevada materially harm and demean same-sex couples and their children."[47]

According to the defendants, the arrival of lesbian and gay marriage would greatly diminish the potency of gendered role-modeling:

> Governor Otter and the Coalition, but not the state of Idaho, also argue that children should be raised by both a male parent and a female parent. They assert that their marriage laws have "recognized, valorized and made normative the roles of 'mother' and 'father' and their uniting, complementary roles in raising their offspring," and insist that allowing same-

> sex couples to marry would send the message that "men and women are interchangeable [and that a] child does not need a mother and a father."[48]

In contrast to Judge Posner's more essentialist rendering, Judge Reinhardt here engages with, and dismisses, an argument that is constructivist in the same ways as the court's analysis in *Baehr*: it assumes gender to be a set of behaviors passed on from one generation to the next through role-modeling. The argument, as framed in the passage, also echoes the often-noted concern that lesbian and gay marriage will lead to an increase in fatherlessness. Judge Reinhardt refutes these arguments bluntly, arguing that allowing lesbian and gay couples to become parents and then to label their families as "second-class" is "cruel as well as unconstitutional." Such reasoning not only fails to survive heightened scrutiny but also runs afoul of the U.S. Supreme Court's precedents holding that sex role stereotypes are impermissible justifications for discrimination.[49]

The court's opinion in *Latta* also puts heterosexuality on trial, asserting that if the states wanted to ensure that the maximum number of children had married parents, they would rescind the right to no-fault divorce or disallow divorce altogether. Moreover, the court observed that if that states wanted to increase the number of children being raised by their biological parents, they would prohibit assisted reproductive technologies and adoption by all couples as well as by single people. Neither state, the court noted, does any of these things.[50] Further elaborating on the disingenuousness of the states' claims, the court observed, "Nevada has been a veritable pioneer in changing these practices, enacting (and benefitting economically from) laws that made it among the easiest places in the country to get married and un-married."[51] In his concurring opinion Judge Reinhardt further develops the point by refuting the defendants' claims that changing the definition of marriage will lead down a slippery slope to incest, polygamy, and child marriage: "Although such claims are not before us, it is not difficult to envision that states could proffer substantially more compelling justifications for such laws than have been put forward in support of the same-sex marriage bans at issue here."[52] These rebuttals to the procreation argument expose some of its most damning potential. Not only do they further illuminate how the argument is illogical and contradictory, but taken seriously and to its fullest extent, the procreation argument would infringe upon the sexual and procreative freedom of everyone, and the damage would fall hardest on straight people.

Judge Berzon's concurring opinion endorses the arguments put forward in the court opinion as well as those of Judge Reinhardt. She writes separately, however, in order to underscore and elaborate on the ways in which bans on lesbian and gay marriage fail constitutional tests of gender discrimination. Echoing the insights of Katherine Franke (whom she cites with reference to the distinctions between sex and gender), Judge Berzon is also concerned that the marriage debate has altered our understanding of the rights-bearing subject. As Franke observes, the marriage debate has, in potentially problematic ways, made the couple the rights-bearing subject rather than the individual.[53] For Judge Berzon laws that "strip *individuals* of their rights or restrict personal choices or opportunities solely on the basis of the individuals' gender are sex discriminatory and must be subjected to intermediate scrutiny."[54] Judge Berzon's opinion draws from the well-developed body of historical, feminist scholarship critiquing gender roles, the family, and women's subordination. Artfully linking these to the present debate, she asserts that the bans are grounded in gender stereotypes about how men and women behave and contribute to marriage, child rearing, and family. In these passages she also takes note of the historically skewed nature of gender relations in marriage. Her comprehensive treatment of the issue highlights the ways that women were long made unequal by the law of marriage, particularly under the laws of coverture, and that such inequality granted men access to the public sphere of politics, economics, and civic duty while simultaneously allowing them control of women's bodies in the form of domestic labor, sexuality, and reproduction within the private sphere. She underscores the point with reference to familial gender roles:

> As a result of this separate-spheres regime, "'[h]istorically, denial or curtailment of women's employment opportunities has been traceable directly to the pervasive presumption that women are mothers first, and workers second.' . . . Stereotypes about women's domestic roles [we]re reinforced by parallel stereotypes presuming a lack of domestic responsibilities for men."[55]

In contrast to the defendants in the case who put forward their worries about lesbian and gay marriage signaling the onset of genderless marriage, Judge Berzon argues that the place of gender in marriage had already diminished and that its lessening importance is a sign of progress.[56]

In her discussion of the gender complementarity and diversity arguments put forth by the defendants, she quotes from the arguments of Idaho that gender complementarity arises from the fact that there must be specific recognition in the law for the respective roles of mothers and fathers and therefore of their united gender performance as married parents. Meanwhile, she takes note of the coalition's proposal that if diversity in education is a good thing, it is also a benefit to the family. In response to this claim, Judge Berzon observes that if diversity in marriage were the state's goal, it could also mandate that all marriage be between people from different races, religions, national origins, and so forth: "Such an absurd requirement would obviously be unconstitutional."[57]

Judge Berzon's final rebuttal to the defendants' arguments is directed at the thread of the procreation argument that "the traditional marriage institution" or "man-woman marriage" is more child-centric than the "genderless" marriages that would be seen in the marriages of gays and lesbians. In order to succeed, this argument would require evidence that bans on lesbian and gay marriage would somehow prevent single parenting. In her words, "The states thus would have to explain, without reliance on sex-stereotypical notions, why the bans on same-sex marriage advance their interests in inducing more biological parents to marry each other. No such showing has been or can be made." These arguments she characterizes as "oxymoronic" and "utterly unsubstantiated."[58]

Heterosexuality through a Deconstitutive Lens

Although the distinctions were subtle, the *Baehr* court implicitly recognized the differences between sex as a biological, essentialist concept and gender as operating in the realm of culture, interpretation, and meaning. Making this distinction also made it possible to begin analytically disassembling marriage, raising the question of what its core meaning might be. If marriage were to be defined by an inextricable link to procreation, it could be understood as natural, biological, and essentialist, but such an interpretation would define the family primarily by an association with sex. If marriage were instead defined primarily as a mechanism for family formation, it not only could be understood by a primary association that was free from the carnal taint of sex but also could then operate in the domain of culture. Ironically, this shift from the marriage-as-sex construction to the marriage-as-gender construction preserved the sanctity of the family by ultimately paving the way for a significant diminution of the place of gender in the family.

The arguments favoring lesbian and gay marriage crafted by the *Goodridge* majority and the judges who weighed in after it worked to correct for the excesses of the procreation argument in a number of ways. For the *Goodridge* court, marriage was not about regulating sex but instead about providing a stable environment for child rearing. Judge Kline's opinion in the California marriage cases works within the same rhetorical frame but illustrates an even more useful adjustment to the narrative. For Judge Kline the U.S. Supreme Court's jurisprudence on privacy and the family was explicitly not about procreation at all. The right to use contraception, the rights of prisoners to marry, the rejection of the state's interference in the marital relationship because of previous acts of procreation all demonstrated to Judge Kline that marriage had been defined as clearly distinct from procreation. Such rhetorical adjustment was necessary if the cultural value of marriage was to be preserved.

Reaffirming the value of marriage was at the center of the Connecticut court's opinion in *Kerrigan*. As jurisdictions across the country established civil unions and other forms of legal recognition, courts were faced with having to determine if such alternatives could satisfy the needs of lesbian and gay families. This move raised the question of whether or not these new statutory protections brought with them the same level of dignity and respect associated with marriage itself. The *Kerrigan* court's juxtaposition of marriage/heterosexuality with civil unions/homosexuality potently illustrates that the answer was no. Indeed, "if the tables were turned" and straight couples were allowed access to only civil unions, they would surely feel that something significant had been taken away from them. Civil unions and other forms of partner registration paled by comparison to the ancient and timeless institution that marriage is thought to be.

By the time *Baskin* and *Latta* were decided, heterosexuality as seen through the lenses of the procreation argument was beginning to look rather silly, profligate, and fragile. When it first appeared in legal discourse, the procreation argument was simply asserted as fact. As we saw in chapter 2, it was part of a tautological definition of marriage that excluded lesbians and gays with no elaboration or evidence required. But as homosexuality was subjected to increased scrutiny, so was heterosexuality, and, as it turned out upon closer inspection, what became clear were the garish features of a receding worldview.[59] The sex that defined the heterosexual family but which was long kept out of view began to emerge as its defining feature in legal and popular discourse.[60] Rather than exclude lesbian and gay couples from marriage, this increased attention and analysis began to have a deconstitutive effect, leaving courts with two options: exclude lesbian and gay couples from marriage by sexualizing the family and devaluing the institution, or maintain the desexualized family by granting access to lesbian and gay couples.

Gender Socialization and the Elasticity of Childhood

Despite the changing relationship between gender and the family, and the decreasing importance of gender in the marital relationship, gender remains a powerful force. As chapter 1 suggests, reproductive politics, the LGBT movement, and our understanding of childhood sexuality have shifted considerably over the past forty years. I do not want to overstate the case, but it is useful to recall that the earliest lesbian and gay marriage cases and the beginning of the gay rights movement were happening at the same time that *Roe v. Wade* (1973) was moving through American courts. Nearly a decade later, when the U.S. Supreme Court ruled that child pornography was a category of prohibited expression, the specter of child sexual abuse emerged as another site of anxiety about gender. Scattered throughout the opinions examined in this book are glimpses of evidence suggesting that although gender may have become less important insofar as the marital couple is concerned, the relationship between gender and childhood has intensified. Textual materials from both sides of the procreation argument point to anxieties about childhood gender socialization as well as an increasingly elastic conception of childhood, one that expands and contracts to suit the rhetorical needs of the moment. I will develop the argument more fully in the conclusion, but for the moment I want to survey the materials in this chapter and the previous one for evidence of the claim.

Worries about the proper gender socialization of children were seen frequently in television advertisements aimed at the voting public, but they also appeared occasionally in judicial opinions. Justice Zarella's opinion in *Kerrigan* puts it most forcefully. According to him, boys cannot become healthy adult men and girls cannot become healthy adult women without their parents serving as proper role models. Moreover, in his view of things, heterosexuality itself must be taught and transmitted from one generation to the next. Successful propagation of the species, he believes, depends on actively promoting heterosexual marriage. In *Donaldson* and *Jackson* (quoted in chapter 2), readers encounter nearly identical language, arguing that heterosexuality itself—a foundational element of the state and civil society—must be properly performed by married adult parents in order ensure that children carry on the tradition.

Just as marriage rights have extended from the individual to the couple, it seems that childhood has taken on an elasticity that allows it to expand well beyond the confines of youth or, when rhetorical needs warrant, to contract to a point before birth. Many of the passages cited here and in chapter 2 originated with the procreation argument and serve as support for maintaining the link between marriage and procreation. But at the same time, they serve as evidence for another somewhat oxymoronic argument: marriage is timeless, historical, and natural, and yet it must be modeled and taught in order to pass from one generation to the next. On such a reading, "childhood" is the flexible term; it stretches outward in support of the rights of heterosexual parents but contracts as necessary to exclude homosexual ones. In Judge Posner's formulation, children are natural conformists, and their need to know that they are not unlike their peers stretches childhood sideways in order to establish certainty and security among children. The failure of the procreation argument brought heterosexuality into the spotlight in new and potentially problematic ways. Full of holes and logically inconsistent, the argument was deftly dismantled.

4

The Nearest Hippie

In the summer of 2013 the U.S. Supreme Court struck down key provisions of the Defense of Marriage Act with its ruling in *United States v. Windsor*, and in *Hollingsworth v. Perry*, the Court denied standing to antigay activists who sought to defend California's Proposition 8, a referendum that would deny marriage rights to lesbian and gay couples. In the summer of 2015 the Court issued its ruling in *Obergefell v. Hodges* and mandated the issuance of marriage licenses and interstate recognition of lesbian and gay marriages. This chapter explores the opinions of the dissenting justices in these major cases. A primary concern among these dissenters was whether or not the Court should have taken the cases in the first place, but running through their argument is another rhetorical thread: all four dissenters mourned the diminished potency of heterosexual male privilege.

Windsor, *Hollingsworth*, and *Obergefell*

The relationship between Edith Windsor and Thea Spyer began in 1967, forty years before the couple was legally married in Canada. In 2009, Spyer died and left her share of their combined assets to Windsor. At the time, New York State recognized their marriage as valid, but because of DOMA, the federal government did not. Windsor was subsequently billed for more than $363,000 in estate taxes by the Internal Revenue Service. Windsor paid the tax and filed suit. Two lower federal courts found in her favor, striking down relevant sections of DOMA, and by the time the case advanced to the U.S. Supreme Court, the Obama administration, too, agreed with Windsor that the tax was unreasonable. By the time the case had reached the U.S. Supreme Court, the federal government had adopted Windsor's position and publicly stated as much but had not yet issued her a refund.

The Court's decision in *Hollingsworth v. Perry* arrived on the same day as its decision in *Windsor*. That case began after the California Supreme Court had ruled that it was a violation of the state's constitution to deny marriage rights to lesbian and gay couples. Subsequently, the state's voters approved a referendum, Proposition 8, that amended the state's constitution to explicitly prohibit recognition of lesbian and gay marriages. The state supreme court ruled that that amendment was properly enacted. When plaintiffs seeking marriage rights filed suit, state officials refused to defend the law in court; Prop 8 proponents intervened in the litigation. When the proponents of the initiative appealed to the Ninth Circuit, that court certified a question to the California Supreme Court, asking whether the Prop 8 proponents had standing to challenge the state's actions. The California Supreme Court ruled that they did; the Ninth Circuit Court of Appeals agreed. The U.S. Supreme Court reversed that decision in *Hollingsworth*. Although the case marked an important moment in the story of marriage litigation, the Court's opinion focuses almost exclusively on the issue of standing and offers little insight into the cultural value of marriage.

In *Obergefell v. Hodges* the U.S. Supreme Court consolidated the petitions of fourteen lesbian and gay couples and two men whose partners were deceased. The Court invited the litigants to address two central questions: (1) Does the Constitution require states to issue marriage licenses to same-sex couples? and (2) Must states recognize the marriages of lesbian and gay couples performed in other jurisdictions? The Court answered both questions in the affirmative.

Procreation at the Supreme Court

The procreation argument appears in both *Windsor* and *Obergefell*, but its rhetorical effects are rather different than we have seen in lower courts. In *Windsor* specifically, dissenting Justices Roberts and Scalia were primarily concerned with the majority's theory of justiciability, that is, the Court's willingness to have heard and decided the case in the first place, and their treatment of the procreation argument is brief. Yet, for the dissenting members of the Court, procreation is among the central defining features of marriage, and although it appears, it is less developed rhetorically than it was in lower court decisions. I will return to the other elements of their rhetorical strategies below, but for the moment I focus on Justice Alito's treatment of the procreation argument.

Justice Alito's dissent in *Windsor* shares the same primary concerns that animate the dissents of Justices Roberts and Scalia: justiciability. All three justices argue that the Court should not have heard the case in the first place because although Edith Windsor had not yet been given a refund for her overpayment of taxes, she and the executive branch agreed that she was entitled to receive one. According to Justice Alito, Edith Windsor was not merely challenging DOMA or seeking a refund on her taxes; rather, "what she seeks is a holding that enshrines in the Constitution a particular understanding of marriage under which the sex of the partners makes no difference."[1] Moreover, in Justice Alito's interpretation, lesbian and gay couples seeking a right to marry were not asking the state for access to a long-standing institution with a demonstrable history of change. Instead, adopting a position seen as early as *Baehr*, Justice Alito insisted that the plaintiffs were seeking a very new right.

Examining two "competing view of marriage" is a central feature of Justice Alito's dissent.[2] The "first and older" view he refers to as either the traditional or the conjugal view of marriage, defining it as an "intrinsically opposite-sex institution."[3] Citing from the respondent's briefs, Justice Alito anchors this view of marriage to an ancient history: "Until a few decades ago, it was an accepted truth for almost everyone who ever lived, in any society in which marriage existed, that there could be marriage only between participants of different sex." This view of marriage he justifies by turning to the procreation argument: "[M]arriage was created for the purpose of channeling heterosexual intercourse into a structure that supports child rearing." The second view of marriage Justice Alito sketches he refers to as the "consent-based" view of marriage, one that is about emotional commitment and sexual attraction between spouses. Because neither view appears in the Constitution, Justice Alito, in agreement with the other dissenters, thinks the Court should have declined to hear the case. But his greatest ire appears in a footnote that seems to take issue with the very appearance of the question:

> The silence of the Constitution on this question should be enough to end the matter as far as the judiciary is concerned. Yet, Windsor and the United States implicitly ask us to endorse the consent-based view of marriage and to reject the traditional view, thereby arrogating to ourselves the

> power to decide a question that philosophers, historians, social scientists, and theologians are better qualified to explore.

At this point in his dissent, Justice Alito offers readers a revealing footnote that comprises three paragraphs. The first paragraph summarizes the findings of fact offered by Judge Vaughn R. Walker of the U.S. District Court, who garnered a great deal of attention when, after hearing the *Hollingsworth* case, he came out as gay. Justice Alito summarizes the elements of marriage found by the trial court as follows: (1) gendered divisions of labor; (2) women raising children and men providing for the family; (3) recognition and approval of a couple's desire to live together; (4) forming a household and economic partnership; (5) permitting lesbian and gay couples to marry would not affect straight marriages. Justice Alito's scorn—and it is difficult to identify his precise target—appears in the second paragraph, quoted here in its entirety: "At times, the trial reached the heights of parody, as when the trial judge questioned his ability to take into account the views of great thinkers of the past because they were unavailable to testify in person in his courtroom." At this moment it appears that Justice Alito is directing his derision at Judge Walker, but in the third paragraph the scope of his scorn broadens. He notes that as "if this spectacle were not enough," some amici and professors of constitutional law argued that the Supreme Court was "bound to accept such findings of fact" unless they were clearly erroneous. Accepting such findings from a trial court is standard practice, but Justice Alito concludes with a further helping of scorn: "Only an arrogant legal culture that has lost all appreciation of its own limitations could take such a suggestion seriously." We might leave this sentence wondering why Justice Alito is not also part of this same legal culture, but, clearly, his preference for not hearing the case would have set him outside that group because he is not among the "arrogant" ones who would have made the findings of fact Judge Walker did, nor is he among the professors and amici who did their jobs by advocating on behalf of their clients and others appearing before the US Supreme Court. It is also possible to read in his footnote a certain dismay with Judge Walker's disinclination to reach into ancient texts in support of a different outcome. As we will see later, ancient texts provide the foundation for the dissents of Justices Roberts, Scalia, and Thomas. In the closing paragraphs of *Obergefell*, Justice Alito assures readers that the "proper method of interpreting the Constitution" requires the virtues of "self-restraint and humility" rather than such arrogance or a willingness to reach for "noble" ends. Justice Alito knows what marriage is, what it always has been, and he is entitled to assert that perspective as a factually accurate claim albeit one he supports only with reference to his own dissent in *Windsor*.[4]

The remaining paragraphs of Justice Alito's dissenting opinion reiterate a common theme seen throughout this debate: marriage is properly the province of the states, and the Supreme Court should have declined to hear these cases. What might give the reader pause, however, is Justice Alito's conceptualization of the relationship between marriage and the Constitution. Because he sees the American constitutional order as properly leaving such questions to be decided by the people, he "would not presume to enshrine either [the traditional/conjugal or consent-based] vision of marriage in our constitutional jurisprudence." The oddity of this claim is that the former view of marriage—what he calls the traditional or conjugal view—has been enshrined in constitutional jurisprudence for a very long time. In *Obergefell*, Justice Scalia observes that the Court majority sees "what lesser legal minds" had previously missed, minds like those of "Thomas Cooley, John Marshall Harlan, Oliver Wendell Holmes, Jr., Learned Hand, Louis Brandeis, William Howard Taft, Benjamin Cardozo, Hugo Black, Felix Frankfurter, Robert Jackson and Henry Friendly."[5] For these dissents, marriage is not only the proper province of the states but also the proper province of theorists, scholars, and writers who were little influenced by feminism or other contributions to scholarship that document changes in the gender, sexuality, or reproductive possibilities associated with marriage. Such a rhetorical move would have set the Court's jurisprudence in an era when homosexuality did not yet exist as part of the social ordering of sexuality. Depending for support from texts that were inherently silent on the subject would have preserved heterosexual privilege through the contemporary perpetuation of such silence.

Because *Windsor* was a tax case involving a challenge to DOMA, the justices were parsimonious in their use of the procreation argument. In *Obergefell*, however, the Court entertained a direct challenge to the exclusion of lesbian and gay couples from marriage, and thus the procreation argument assumed a larger role. For Justice Roberts the "universal definition of marriage as the union of a man and a woman is no historical coincidence." It came about not as the result of a "political movement, discovery, disease, war, religious doctrine," or other force of history. Moreover, it did not result from some "prehistoric decision to exclude gays and lesbians." For Justice Roberts, marriage "arose in the nature of things to meet a vital need: ensuring that children are conceived by a mother and father committed to raising them in the stable conditions of a lifelong relationship."[6] As we saw in chapters 2 and 3, lower courts had quite a bit to say about the procreation argument and its shortcomings. Justice Alito remained unconvinced:

> The premises supporting this concept of marriage are so fundamental that they rarely require articulation. The human race must procreate to survive. Procreation occurs through sexual relations between a man and a woman. When sexual relations result in the conception of a child, that child's prospects are generally better if the mother and father stay together rather than going their separate ways. Therefore, for the good of children and society, sexual relations that can lead to procreation should occur only between a man and a woman committed to a lasting bond.[7]

Throughout his opinion, Justice Roberts avoids or ignores the question of how denying marriage rights to lesbian and gay couples might be a benefit to the children of either lesbian/gay or straight couples; it is the argument that none of the antimarriage voices can address because there is no logical answer to it. Although Justice Roberts here adopts a more measured version of the procreation argument than we saw in earlier chapters, it is clear that regulating sex is more important to him than providing for children. The preceding passage takes a very restrictive view of sexuality but leaves significant room for negotiation. The "sexual relations that can lead to procreation" are very limited in number; there is exactly one such act, but for Justice Roberts, that one act establishes a "biologically rooted" definition of marriage. These conceptions of marriage he anchors with citations to Blackstone, Locke, and more notably Noah Webster, whose first dictionary of the English language, published in 1828, Justice Roberts cites as support for the definition of marriage as "legal union of a man and a woman for life" and also as "serv[ing] the purposes of 'preventing the promiscuous intercourse of the sexes.'"[8] Regardless of the authority we might ascribe to Webster's dictionary, neither of these statements is exactly accurate. Marriage may have long united only men and women, but divorce has been available to them throughout American history. Additionally, because marriage has always been part of the American legal landscape, we can never know if a society without marriage would have been any more or less promiscuous than the one we live in.

Justice Alito's dissenting opinion in *Obergefell* makes clear that, for him, marriage and procreation are inseparable parts of a single construct. Embarking from the premise that straight marriage is a fundamental right while lesbian and gay marriage is something else, something new and problematic, Justice Alito writes that it is "beyond dispute" that what the plaintiffs sought in *Obergefell* was not among the rights protected by the Constitution. He supports the point with a citation to his dissenting opinion in *Windsor* suggesting that his definition of marriage is the only one readers will require.

Justice Alito's summary of the majority opinion is perhaps most notable for what it overlooks. He finds in Justice Kennedy's opinion that marriage is designed to "promote the well-being" of people who opt to marry; that it provides "emotional fulfillment"; and that it "benefits society" as a whole by inspiring people to live in "stable, fulfilling, and supportive" relationships.[9] This conception of marriage he describes as being focused "entirely on the happiness of persons who choose to marry," but it is at odds with Justice Alito's beliefs about marriage because it overlooks the essential element of procreation. In the subsequent paragraph he describes the states' defense of their bans on lesbian and gay marriage and finds that such laws are intended to promote the "best atmosphere for raising children" but warns that this "traditional" conception of marriage may not be recognizable to many people: "If this traditional understanding of the purpose of marriage does not ring true to all ears today, that is probably because the tie between marriage and procreation has frayed. Today, for instance, more than 40% of all children in this country are born to unmarried women." This change, he offers, is both the cause and the result of changing views about marriage and may have other pernicious consequences as yet to be predicted.

There are several omissions from Justice Alito's description that merit attention. One of the primary reasons lesbian and gay couples want to marry is to provide stable, supportive environments for their children whose interests are overlooked by his conception of marriage. More important, perhaps, is the characterization of marriage as a "frayed" institution and the causes Justice Alito attributes to it. Judge Berzon's opinion in *Latta v. Otter*, discussed in chapter 3, and much other scholarship cited throughout this debate make it clear that marriage has, indeed, changed across the course of American history, and many of those changes have happened in the interests of gender equity. The demise of coverture, the rise of no-fault divorce, and greater attention to the economic consequences of divorce and single parenting have made marriage a less risky proposition for women, changes that might be understood as positive developments rather than as symptoms of an institution in tatters. It is especially noteworthy that Justice Alito identifies the growing number of children born to unmarried women as both the "cause and result" of changes in the way marriage is understood. Why, we should ask, are the births he references attributed to women and not to parents? The numbers of children born to unmarried women have increased, but many of those women live with the fathers of their children in stable, familial settings. Additionally, as the marriage debate makes abundantly clear, many of those children were also born to lesbian couples who were actively prohibited from marrying. The choice of "women" invokes the trope of single motherhood and thereby excuses men from blame in what Justice Alito sees as the fraying of marriage. Foregrounding women as the source of illegitimate births should also be read as an attempt to preserve male, heterosexual privilege by occluding the fact that such children also have fathers.

Power, Prejudice, and Liberty

In *The Limits to Union: Same-Sex Marriage and the Politics of Civil Rights*, Jonathan Goldberg-Hiller writes:

> The struggle over same-sex marriage is a prism that splits citizenship and sovereignty. No longer seen in the white light and shadow of juridical relations, the demands for formal recognition on the basis of private lives

> has refracted citizenship into its many governmentalized components—the discursive spectrum of the new sovereign.[10]

As he argues throughout the book, the marriage debates indicate that citizenship is about civil rights as well as economics, national security, processes of civilization, tradition, and space. Seeing sovereignty through this prism reveals how its various components operate. In its most basic form the procreation argument locates marriage as the point of intersection between the family and the nation; thus the family not only serves as the founding metaphor for the nation but also allows the nation to be understood as a form of social order wherein difference can be organized hierarchically, that is, a location wherein women are subordinate to men and children to adults. Katherine Franke's work shows how marriage has been used to promote and sustain racial hierarchy.[11] Such hierarchical ordering of society is rhetorically positioned as natural, essentialist, and biologically ordained. The dissenting justices in *Windsor* and *Obergefell* drafted opinions that strive to return our conceptions of sovereignty and citizenship to an earlier era in American history, an era when such "natural" hierarchies allocated power and privilege in a way that was unquestioned if not also regularly unnoticed by elites.

Three themes at the center of these dissenting opinions—power, prejudice, and liberty—suggest that as the procreation argument began failing in lower courtrooms and could no longer naturalize older social hierarchies, the justices took umbrage at the newly equilibrated social hierarchy. Their concerns with power, bound up with their theories of justiciability, express more than a passing concern with who it is that gets to decide on the ordering of social life. Each opinion, in its own way, is a rhetorical attempt to reconstitute a social order wherein the white male head of a household is also the representative of the family in civic life, a revival of coverture for another era. The dissenters' concerns with prejudice stem from their new position in the social order, one that because of diminished privilege has the potential to spotlight their prejudices. Aligning themselves with allegedly pro-family, antigay religious groups, the dissenters resent the possibility that their prejudices, previously expressed without censorship, might be silenced. Finally, this dislocation from positions of power coupled with the threat of prejudice invites the dissenters to worry about how liberty is allocated in the new social order.

Power

Justice Scalia's dissents in *Windsor* and *Obergefell* echo a common theme from his jurisprudential philosophy, that is, he prefers that the Court's decisions be historically grounded in textual authority. Decisions that fail to do so, in his opinion, are a threat to our democratic system of government. For Justice Scalia, more than any of the other dissenters, these marriage cases were about power, but it is not only the Court's institutional power that he laments. That is, of course, the literal manifestation of his concerns, but each justice, in his own way, is also clearly troubled by what *Windsor* portends insofar as the majority opinion has now included gays and lesbians in the fullness of American citizenship. Justice Scalia's dissenting opinion opens with the following:

> This case is about power in several respects. It is about the power of our people to govern themselves, and the power of this Court to pronounce the law. Today's opinion aggrandizes the latter, with the predictable consequence of diminishing the former. We have no power to decide this case. And even if we did, we have no power under the Constitution to invalidate this democratically adopted legislation. The Court's errors on both points spring forth from the same diseased root: an exalted conception of the role of this institution in America.

In characteristically colorful language, Justice Scalia proceeds to assail the motives of his colleagues in the majority, accusing them of being "eager" and "*hungry*" (his emphasis) to announce their views on marriage and ignoring appropriate rules of justiciability in order to do so. Rather than frame his analysis in the technical language of the law, Justice Scalia sarcastically characterizes the problem as of little interest to "anyone but the people of We the People," and the claim here cuts in two directions at once. His preferred formulation would deny that Edith Windsor is among the people of "We the People"; he would establish an exclusionary framework that places her—along with all other gays and lesbians—outside the full measure of citizenship that he enjoyed.

At the same time that Edith Windsor has moved into the inner circle of American citizenship, Justice Scalia has been placed on par with her, and he was not happy about it.

In the opening paragraphs of his dissent in *Obergefell*, Justice Scalia assures readers twice that "the substance of today's decree is not of immense personal importance to me"; that the law can recognize whatever it prefers regarding living arrangements, tax benefits, or rights of inheritance; and that such recognition "is not of special importance to me."[12] His claims that the substance of the decision is not of "immense" or "special" importance to him reads as disingenuous given his long-standing opposition to gay rights; it mattered a great deal to him. The real force of his complaint was summed up as follows: "It is of overwhelming importance, however, who it is that rules me. Today's decree says that my Ruler, and the Ruler of 320 million Americans coast-to-coast, is a majority of the nine lawyers on the Supreme Court."[13] Although Justice Scalia's primary concern in this passage is the majority's willingness to have heard the case in the first place, there is an undeniably personal quality to the offense expressed. The Court's rulings minimize the role Justice Scalia himself played as one of the People who got to decide what marriage is. Social hierarchies have been realigned, and he is no longer among the rulers whose preferred structures dominate. The decision is about power, and Justice Scalia's position of social and political power has been destabilized in part because it has been called into question and refused.

This exclusion from the People who get to determine how social power is allocated is a problem for all of the dissenting justices, and each, in his own way, takes umbrage at the majority opinions. For Justice Scalia, the People were right to draft and enact DOMA and to prohibit lesbian and gay marriages. He would have preferred that the Court disavow the power to decide both cases, a move that would preserve the Court's ability to sustain what Justice Scalia deems an appropriate form of power. Prior to these decisions he was one of the People, part of the majority whose monopoly on the power to define family was ruptured by *Windsor* and put to rest in *Obergefell*; being incorporated into the same conceptualization of sovereignty and citizenship as the gay and lesbian plaintiffs in these cases diminishes his male, heterosexual privilege.

Justice Scalia's worries resonate in the opinions of Justices Roberts and Alito. Justice Roberts's opinion in *Windsor* is also concerned with jurisdiction, and much of his text is committed to developing his theory of justiciability. He opens by claiming agreement with Justice Scalia's two main points, and he, too, is worried about who the People are and whether he is still included among them. Like Justice Scalia, he takes offense at the majority's characterization of DOMA, decrying their inclination to see a "sinister motive" in that legislation, one coupled with a "bare desire to harm," a determination that he contests by stating that he would not tar the legislative branch with the "brush of bigotry." Moreover, he finds the "banal title" of DOMA to signify nothing; the text of DOMA and the congressional record of its passage belie the claim. In one of his more colorful moments, Justice Scalia refutes the majority's assertion that marriage is among the freedoms guaranteed by the Constitution. Indeed, he characterizes freedom of intimacy as being "abridged rather than expanded by marriage." In a moment that harkens back to another moment long past, Justice Scalia suggests that if readers have any doubt about the restrictiveness of marriage, they need only "[a] sk the nearest hippie."

Justice Alito's opinion addresses the issue of justiciability and takes direct aim at the changing conceptualization of family portended by the decision. Like Justice Scalia, Justice Alito sets aside the fact that the people of New York extended marriage rights to lesbian and gay couples through the state's legislature and that Windsor challenged federal intrusion into what has long been understood as the proper domain of the states. As with Justices Scalia and Roberts, Justice Alito is also concerned about how Windsor has expanded the definition of the People: "In our system of government, ultimate sovereignty rests with the people, and the people have the right to control their own destiny. Any change on a question so fundamental should be made by the people through their elected officials."[14] Justice Alito is here worried about including gays and lesbians among the People. Again, this seems to underscore the problem outlined earlier; the state of New York recognized the marriage of Windsor and Spyer, and it is the federal government that subsequently refused to apply appropriate tax law.

Justices Scalia, Roberts, and Alito see themselves as having been excluded from a national community where people like themselves are entitled to the privileges of membership, and they also saw themselves as endowed with the power to determine the rules of membership in that community. By articulating their concerns with power, the dissenting justices each strive to reconstitute and naturalize their preferred power hierarchy, and, ironically, they would have preferred to achieve this goal by refusing to hear the cases before them. They would maintain their privilege and monopoly on power by refusing to exercise that power and maintaining the silence surrounding their decision.

But that is not the only irony on display in these cases. Justice Roberts's dissent in *Obergefell* relies extensively on *Lochner v. New York* (1905), wherein a majority of the Supreme Court struck down a New York state law, drafted to protect public health, limiting the number of hours bakery employees could be required to work. *Lochner* has long been held out not only as incorrect in result but as an example of the Court inappropriately acting as a superlegislature and second-guessing the better judgment of an elected body under the guise of protecting a liberty of contract. Justice Roberts's dissent draws on this discredited moment in jurisprudential history. In an effort to align himself with the dissenting justices in *Lochner*, most notably Justice Holmes, Justice Roberts accuses the *Obergefell* majority of overstepping the proper bounds of its authority. Justice Roberts intends to align himself with the vindicated dissenters in *Lochner*, but the alignment does more work than he may have intended. In *Lochner* a politically conservative majority struck down a progressive state law intended to protect the health and safety of employees, and it did so, ostensibly, by preserving their liberty to form contracts with their employers: damaging, lopsided contracts. In *Obergefell* a progressive majority of the Court struck down conservative state statutes that excluded lesbian and gay couples from the protections of marriage, thereby extending to that segment of the population a liberty of contract they had not previously enjoyed. This attempt to cloak himself in the mantle of constitutional righteousness succeeds at first glance, but the analogy is flawed. *Lochner* has been discredited not only because it exemplifies jurisprudential overreach by the Court but because it struck down a law intended to protect the powerless (bakery employees) from more powerful forces (bakery owners/employers). In *Obergefell*, the majority protected a minority group with limited political power (i.e., gays and lesbians) from discriminatory laws *and* protected their liberty of contract.

Justice Roberts's use of citation seems more on point when he writes that the Supreme Court's decisions "have consistently refused to allow litigants to convert the shield provided by constitutional liberties into a sword to demand positive entitlements from the State." To support this proposition he cites *DeShaney v. Winnebago County* (1989).[15] In that case a young child was beaten into a vegetative state by his abusive father despite the mother's pleas for assistance from the state's department of social services. Justice Roberts's invocation of the case is intended to support the notion that despite the state's creation of institutions and procedures designed to achieve a laudable goal, citizens are not entitled to expect success. It would press the point to absurdity to suggest that Justice Roberts sees marriage contracts as lopsided or damaging or to intimate that his interpretation of gays and lesbians is an infantilizing one. Nonetheless, what can be taken from his use of these citations is that he, like Justice Scalia, is striving to reconstitute a dominant, powerful community, one in which people like him have a monopoly. Like the Founding Fathers, or the list of exceptional legal minds Justice Scalia listed, the dissenters are entitled to make choices, establish policy, and extend benefits—or not. Their vision of the power of a paternalistic state would be maintained through the refusal to exercise that power, but in these cases, their place atop the social order has been compromised.

Prejudice

The dissenters' preferred jurisprudence reaches backward through history and draws voices from the past into the present, voices that were largely silent on matters of sexual orientation. Just as the procreation argument called into view the garish features of heterosexuality, the dissenters' opinions in *Windsor* and *Obergefell* put on display the garish features of the justices' conception of social order. Having been displaced as the dominant voices of authority, they express considerable concern over what that displacement might mean. Of particular worry to the dissenters is that the decisions would silence the sincerely held religious beliefs of those opposed to lesbian and gay marriage. Justice Kennedy's majority opinion in *Obergefell* is mindful of the point:

> Many who deem same-sex marriage to be wrong reach that conclusion based on decent and honorable religious or philosophical premises, and neither they nor their beliefs are disparaged here. But when that sincere, personal opposition becomes enacted law and public policy, the necessary consequence is to put the imprimatur of the State itself on an exclusion that soon demeans or stigmatizes those whose own liberty is then denied.[16]

Similar language appears throughout Justice Kennedy's opinions in both *Windsor* and *Obergefell.* Legally preventing the marriages of same-sex couples "demeans" couples and their children; it "humiliates" their children; DOMA "seeks to injure" or "harm" a "politically unpopular group" and to "write inequality" into U.S. law.

This characterization is troubling to Justice Scalia, and he pushes the measured language of Justice Kennedy's opinion to shrill extremes. "The majority concludes that the only motive for [DOMA] was the 'bare . . . desire to harm a politically unpopular group.'"[17] They acted with "hateful hearts," they were "mean-spirited," "unhinged members of a wild-eyed lynch mob." He continues:

> [T]he majority says that the supporters of this Act acted with *malice*—with *the "purpose"* "to disparage and to injure" same-sex couples. It says that the motivation for DOMA was to "demean," to "impose inequality," to "impose . . . a stigma," to deny people "equal dignity," to brand gay people as "unworthy," and to "*humiliat*[*e*]" their children.
>
> I am sure these accusations are quite untrue. To be sure (as the majority points out), the legislation is called the Defense of Marriage Act. But to defend traditional marriage is not to condemn, demean, or humiliate those who would prefer other arrangements, any more than to defend the Constitution of the United States is to condemn, demean, or humiliate other constitutions. To hurl such accusations so casually demeans *this institution*. . . . It is one thing for a society to elect change; it is another for a court of law to impose change by adjudging those who oppose it *hostes humani generis*, enemies of the human race.[18]

Despite Justice Scalia's certainty regarding the veracity of these claims, his characterization of the majority's interpretation of DOMA avoids the act's legislative history and purpose, a tendency seen throughout his career. Meanwhile, the majority opinion specifically references the legislative history and text of DOMA. Justice Scalia disagrees with the majority's assertion that DOMA was enacted out of a bare desire to harm lesbian and gay couples, but that interpretation is the one most obvious to even a casual reader of the *Congressional Record*:

> Before discussing the Hawaiian lawsuit, the Committee believes it is important to place that development in its larger context. In particular, it is critical to understand the nature of the orchestrated legal assault being waged against traditional heterosexual marriage by gay rights groups and their lawyers. Only then can the Committee's concerns that motivated H.R. 3396 [DOMA] be fully explained and understood.[19]

The legislative history and text of DOMA inarguably depict lesbian and gay marriage as a threat being advanced by a dangerous enemy that must be stopped from destroying a sacred institution. Justice Scalia's flawed analogy exposes the problems with his argument: defending the U.S. Constitution does not require a refusal to recognize the constitutions of other nations, and recognizing foreign constitutions does not imply an assault on the Constitution of the United States. DOMA was nothing if not a refusal to recognize legitimate marriages coupled with a belief that some marriages were an assault on others. Moreover, he overlooked the fact that Edith Windsor and Thea Spyer were residents of New York, a state that made marriage rights available to them through the legislative process. Ergo, we should pause to ask: Who are the People that worry Justice Scalia? On the surface his primary concern is with representative democracy and a conceptualization of the People as a whole. But we might ask whether he counts himself among the people who passed DOMA, or the people who vote in New York. He is very explicit about the fact that he would like to have seen the ruling confined to the New York district court that heard it first, a position that would comport with his views of federalism but one that would cause him some conflict given New York's pro-gay policy at issue. But in this moment, and contrary to his preference for states' rights arguments, Justice Scalia clearly prefers that political power should emanate from the federal government such that DOMA would trump New York state law.

Justice Scalia's hyperbolic recharacterization of Justice Kennedy's opinion in *Windsor* does at least two notable things. First, when he claims that "these accusations are quite untrue," he denies the undeniable motivations behind congressional enactment of DOMA. The act was drafted specifically to maintain the second-class status of lesbian and gay relationships. Injury, the imposition of stigma, denial of equal dignity, and sustaining the belief that gay and lesbian people are unworthy of marriage were precisely the motivations behind the act, but Justice Scalia pushes these characterizations further. Justice Kennedy has not accused anyone of being mean-spirited or of acting with hateful hearts, and suggesting that he sees those opposed to lesbian and gay marriage as wild-eyed, unhinged members of a lynch mob belittles the damaging effect that DOMA had on Windsor and Spyer just as it did thousands of other married couples. The rhetorical adjustment Justice Scalia tried to effectuate in this passage would have reduced DOMA to a benign and sensible policy.

Second, having made this rhetorical adjustment, Justice Scalia can then depict himself, and others who share his point of view, as having been unfairly maligned and silenced, his privilege wounded: "It is hard to admit that one's political opponents are not monsters, especially in a struggle like this one, and the challenge in the end proves more than today's Court can handle. Too bad."[20] Bristling with offense, Justice Scalia strove to reconstitute the faded majority that once opposed lesbian and gay marriage and to include himself among the unfortunates who, in the face of the *Windsor* decision, may be forced to contain or suppress their animus. Justice Alito shares this concern. In his depiction of Windsor's claim, he writes that accepting the plaintiff's argument "would cast all those who cling to traditional beliefs about the nature of marriage in the role of bigots or superstitious fools."[21] His dissent in *Obergefell* sums up these worries: "I assume that those who cling to old beliefs will be able to whisper their thoughts in the recesses of their homes, but if they repeat those views in public they will risk being labeled as bigots and treated as such by governments, employers, and schools."[22] What these dissenting justices fear most is the inversion of social power and dignity that has been wrought throughout the marriage debate. As generations of queer scholarship have demonstrated, breaking the silences of the closet has been key to political advancement for lesbians and gays. Never before have these justices, like many other Americans, had to justify their own prejudices because, previously, those prejudices were understood as commonsense expressions of well-known truths. These changes in the social, cultural, and political relationships between homo- and heterosexuality are moving those opposed to homosexuality into a closet of homophobic silence, and it is a space they find unfamiliar and confining.

Liberty

In her book *Wedlocked: The Perils of Marriage Equality*, law professor Katherine Franke juxtaposes the advent of marriage rights for gays and lesbians today with the extension of marriage rights to newly freed blacks during Reconstruction. As she demonstrates, "The gay rights movement has rebranded itself as no longer about the right to non-normative sex and sexuality but rather about the dignity of gay families and kin who share a normative similarity to heterosexuals and the nuclear family." She continues: "In ways that few of us would have imagined only a dozen years ago, homosexuals have escaped the curse of Sodom much more readily and successfully than have African Americans the curse of Ham."[23] This process of rebranding has occurred in large part because the procreation argument threatened to rebrand heterosexuality in a manner that exposed its problematic features. Better that gays and lesbians become legally straight than to risk damaging the cultural value of marriage. But while this process has been one of redemption for gays and lesbians, it has been something else for African Americans. Indeed, the marriage movement relied on what Franke calls a "gay Moynihan moment," and that is a large part of the problem that concerns her. Rather than fight for the rights of single parents or illegitimate children, plaintiffs in the lesbian and gay marriage cases frequently relied on the stigma associated with illegitimacy and single parenting in order to convince courts that the children of gays and lesbians deserved married parents. Franke shows readers throughout the book that the multiple and varied family forms associated with African Americans have resulted from the way marriage rights were extended to newly freed slaves during Reconstruction. Consequently, pathologizing such family forms racializes "alternative" family forms in a problematic manner. As Franke observes, "[W]hether in the nineteenth century or today, marriage has by and large served as a test [African Americans] are doomed to fail."[24]

Justice Thomas's dissents in the marriage cases invite us to read them ironically. We might begin by revisiting his opinion from *Lawrence v. Texas* (2003). In his dissent there, Justice Thomas wrote that although he found the law uncommonly silly, he could not find in the Bill of Rights, or in any other part of the Constitution, a general right of privacy or, "as the Court terms it today, the 'liberty of the person both in its spatial and more transcendent dimensions.'"[25] Justice Thomas's dissent in *Obergefell* is structured around the concept of liberty, and he begins by insisting that liberty is best understood as "freedom from government action, not entitlement to government benefits." Moreover, as he points out, liberty does not stand alone in the Constitution as a substantive right, only as something that cannot be taken away from citizens without first affording them due process. Liberty, as he defines it with citation to Blackstone, refers to "the power of loco-motion, of changing situation, or removing one's person to whatsoever place one's own inclination may direct; without imprisonment or restraint, unless by due course of law."[26] This notion of negative liberty seems, at first glance, to reference freedom from the threat of state punishment: "As a philosophical matter, liberty is only freedom from governmental action, not an entitlement to governmental benefits. And as a constitutional matter, it is likely even narrower than that, encompassing only freedom from physical restraint and imprisonment."

In its literal form Justice Thomas's preferred conception of liberty involves little more than freedom from the threat of punishment by the state, but it stops there. Liberty, for Justice Thomas, cannot also involve entitlements to claim government benefits, and, like Justice Alito, he knows what marriage is and always has been. He writes: "Petitioners misunderstand the institution of marriage when they say that it would 'mean little' absent governmental recognition."[27] He goes on to explain that *Loving*, *Turner*, and *Zablocki* were not about requiring the state to recognize certain forms of marriage but instead involved "absolute prohibitions on private actions." Although his phrasing is somewhat opaque, it seems for a moment to reference criminal sanctions. State penalties were at issue in both *Loving* and *Zablocki*, but in *Turner* the state's actions would have required obtaining a prison warden's permission before an inmate could marry. The plaintiffs in *Obergefell*, Justice Thomas concludes, were not threatened by the state but instead were asking for state recognition. While this may distinguish *Obergefell* from *Loving* and *Zablocki*, the logic of the argument appears to unravel in the face of *Turner*. In that case plaintiffs sought the right to marry and were denied it until the Supreme Court intervened.

Justice Thomas, like many others, was also concerned about what the decision portended for religious liberty, but this section of his dissent lacks any specific examples of how religious liberty might be threatened by the Court's decision. After sketching a history of religious liberty and the protections afforded to religious practice, Justice Thomas turns his attention to the amicus briefs submitted in the case. There he notes that marriage is both a governmental and a religious institution. The latter, he opines, is threatened by the decision, making it "inevitable that the two will come into conflict as individuals and churches are confronted with demands to participate in and endorse civil marriages between same-sex couples." But the passages in this section of the opinion are thin on specificity, and their logic is rather cloudy. The key to understanding Justice Thomas's concerns is this: "Religious liberty is about more than just the protection for 'religious organizations and persons . . . as they seek to teach the principles that are so fulfilling and so central to their lives and faiths.'" Absent any clear link between recognizing lesbian and gay marriages and an imposition on religious liberty, readers are left to ponder what the allusive passage might mean. It seems that Justice Thomas is concerned that when states recognize lesbian and gay marriages, that act in and of itself contradicts the sentiments espoused by some religious institutions. On this score his worry is about the message sent by state approval of lesbian and gay marriages. But given the fact that Justice Thomas's conception of liberty emphasizes freedom from government restraint, the interpretation invites an ironic reading. His conception of liberty would prohibit lesbian and gay couples from asking for state recognition, but although granting such recognition is a problem for religious exercise, it does not compromise religious dignity:

> The majority's musings are thus deeply misguided, but at least those musings can have no effect on the dignity of the persons the majority demeans. Its mischaracterization of the arguments presented by the States and their

> amici can have no effect on the dignity of those litigants. Its rejection of laws preserving the traditional definition of marriage can have no effect on the dignity of the people who voted for them. Its invalidation of those laws can have no effect on the dignity of the people who continue to adhere to the traditional definition of marriage. And its disdain for the understandings of liberty and dignity upon which this Nation was founded can have no effect on the dignity of Americans who continue to believe in them.

Given this, it would seem that Justice Thomas has no grounds for his own worries, but the passage is confusing, particularly the opening sentence: Who has the majority demeaned if the Court can have no effect on their dignity? The remainder of the passage invites readers to recognize the ironic conflicts between an inability to demean and a diminution of the dignity of those who voted for DOMA.

Justice Roberts's worries about liberty were also built on a foundation of religious belief and practice. Following the same line of logic noted earlier, he faults the majority for pointing out that religious institutions may continue to teach whatever they like regarding marriage, but he, too, is concerned about free exercise. Unlike Justice Thomas, he offers some hypothetical specifics such as when religious universities allow only straight, married couples access to campus housing or when religious adoption agencies express a preference for placing children with straight couples. Here again we see worries about the silencing of antigay animus and the loss of privilege accompanying it.

Sora Han's *Letters of the Law* examines what she calls the fantasy of color blindness that haunts American constitutional jurisprudence.[28] Han argues that American jurisprudence has roots in slavery but that our official discourse "apostrophizes" race, dropping it out of sight when it threatens to undermine other ways of knowing. She uses *Lawrence v. Texas* (2003) to illustrate the point. *Lawrence* ultimately resulted in the Supreme Court striking down sodomy laws on a national scale, but it began with a false police report called in by the jealous boyfriend of Tyrone Garner, Lawrence's sexual partner. In that case the jealous boyfriend reported a "nigger going crazy with a gun" in order to capture the attention of the cops. Han argues that the case "apostrophizes" race and draws meaning from the fantasy of color blindness; *Lawrence* was a problem for sexual privacy because it threatened the property right that is white male sexuality, and the racial element of the case dropped out of view in the same way that the dissenting justices hoped to keep heterosexual privilege quiet.

Among the more striking aspects of Justice Thomas's dissent is its reliance on a similar strategy of "apostrophizing." After faulting the majority opinion for asserting that marriage could confer dignity on lesbian and gay couples, he writes, "The flaw in that reasoning, of course, is that the Constitution contains no 'dignity' Clause, and even if it did, the government would be incapable of bestowing dignity." Human dignity, Justice Thomas asserts, is innate:

> Slaves did not lose their dignity (any more than they lost their humanity) because the government allowed them to be enslaved. Those held in internment camps did not lose their dignity because the government confined them. And those denied governmental benefits certainly do not lose their dignity because the government denies them those benefits. The government cannot bestow dignity, and it cannot take it away.

Although Justice Thomas is vague with respect to what dangers *Obergefell* may portend for religious institutions, he gestures toward a racialized interpretation in a footnote. There he reminds readers that before *Loving*, religious officials who chose to perform marriage ceremonies for interracial couples were subject to criminal penalties, an ironic comment given that in an earlier footnote he states: "The suggestion of petitioners and their amici that antimiscegenation laws are akin to laws defining marriage as between one man and one woman is both offensive and inaccurate." After tracing antimiscegenation laws back to the history of slavery, Justice Thomas observes that laws banning lesbian and gay marriage do not share this sordid history. He is quite correct on this point. What he overlooks is the fact that slavery and homophobia were not contemporaneous historical constructs; the former predates the latter. Gender and the history of sexism, which he largely ignores, would have made the better analogy.

The relationship between sexual orientation and race appears throughout the marriage debate and is seen most clearly when it invites analogies to *Loving*. Justice Thomas finds the analogy offensive and inaccurate, and for a moment the reader might understand his racial identity to be the source of his offense. Such a conclusion would be premature. When Justice Thomas explains that constitutional liberty refers to the power of locomotion or movement without imprisonment or restraint, he draws on the language of the Magna Carta to do so: "No freeman shall be taken or imprisoned, or be disseised of his freehold, or liberties, or free customs, or be outlawed, or exiled, or any otherwise destroyed." In his attempt to explicate the importance of "due process" and its connection to "life, liberty, and property," he highlights the connection between the Framers' conception of liberty, the writings of Blackstone, and the constitutions of Maryland, North Carolina, and South Carolina, each of which also explicitly used the phrase "life, liberty, or property" to describe what would not be taken from any "freeman" without due process. Asserting that this conception of liberty was available to "freemen" requires Justice Thomas to apostrophize race in order to remain coherent. The conceptions of liberty Justice Thomas prefers protected a very small segment of the population at the time the Constitution was written, and it was a conception that would not have included him.

While Justice Thomas's conception of liberty and its relationship to *Loving* are somewhat opaque, the formulation offered by Justice Roberts is even more puzzling. Describing *Turner* and *Zablocki*, Justice Roberts writes that the laws challenged in those cases did not define marriage as "the union of a man and a woman, *where neither party owed child support or is in prison*," nor did the ban at issue in *Loving* define marriage as "the union of a man and a woman *of the same race*."[29] After noting that at common law there was no ban on interracial marriage, Justice Roberts informs readers that "[r]emoving racial barriers to marriage therefore did not change what a marriage was any more than integrating schools changed what a school was." In *Windsor*, Justice Alito writes:

> In asking the Court to determine that §3 of DOMA is subject to and violates heightened scrutiny, Windsor and the United States thus ask us to rule that the presence of two members of the opposite sex is as rationally related to marriage as white skin is to voting or a Y-chromosome is to the ability to administer an estate.

Justices Roberts and Alito would have readers begin from the premise that race should not determine a person's fitness for education or to vote and that gender should not determine fitness to administer an estate. But the analogies prove too much. Removing racial barriers to marriage and education fundamentally changed the nature of both institutions in the same way that removing gender from marriage changes marriage; the key to understanding each analogy is reproduction. Prior to *Loving*, miscegenation statutes maintained the whiteness of marriage as an institution. As Justice Thomas points out, miscegenation statutes were designed to keep white women from giving birth to mixed-race children. That black women would continue giving birth to mixed-race children, as they had long been forced to do, was of little concern to anyone. It is similarly inaccurate to assume, as Justice Roberts does, that before *Brown v. Board* schools were not also sites where racial hierarchies were reinscribed on the body politic. *Brown* did, indeed, begin to change what schools are just as *Loving* changed the definition of marriage. Although racial disparities in education are far from over, the *Brown* decision and its implementation were designed to stop the historical tendency by which white supremacy was instantiated through education.

Justice Roberts's discussion of coverture suffers from similar flaws. Although he admits its demise, along with the disappearance of arranged marriages, his admission sits uneasily alongside the comparison he chooses to support his position:

> States have replaced coverture, the doctrine by which a married man and woman became a single legal entity, with laws that respect each participant's separate status. Racial restrictions on marriage, which "arose as an incident to slavery" to promote "White Supremacy," were repealed by many States and ultimately struck down by this Court.

Justice Roberts characterizes the removal of race from the marital equation rather differently from the manner in which he characterizes gender:

> If you had asked a person on the street how marriage was defined, no one would ever have said, "Marriage is the union of a man and a woman, where the woman is subject to coverture." The majority may be right that the "history of marriage is one of both continuity and change," but the core meaning of marriage has endured.[30]

The example illustrates more than Justice Roberts may have intended. Reframing his own chosen hypothetical, it seems unlikely that if anyone had been asked to define marriage, pre-*Loving*, they would have replied that it was a "union of man and woman intended to ensure racial purity." The problem with both hypotheticals, however, is that each assumes engagement with a casual observer because, in both instances, the law specifically stated otherwise regardless of what definitions the casual observer might have offered. The law at issue in *Loving* was clear about its intent just as the laws of coverture were clear about establishing male dominance over women. What Justice Roberts resists with his hypothetical is the possibility that marriage long served as a site where sexism was reproduced and maintained. Lamenting, as he does, the removal of gender from marriage suggests that he and the other dissenters mourn the changing value of gender and the consequent diminution of masculine privilege within the family that it portends.

Heterosexual Privilege Disrupted

While it is too early to know exactly how or even if lesbian and gay marriage will affect broader cultural conceptions of family formation, it is productive to consider how the marriage debate has affected heterosexual privilege. At a historical moment when other forms of privilege—white privilege, male privilege, class privilege—are being regularly called into view in both scholarly work and mainstream media, heterosexual privilege remains an undertheorized and underutilized dimension of analysis. In an insightful article that unpacks the idea of heterosexual privilege, Devon Carbado argues that male feminism—thought by some to be an impossibility or a contradiction in terms—is possible and that it requires men to examine the belief that their identities are "pre-political givens."[31] Gender, he observes, is usually thought of as a category that is synonymous with female, and thus while women's disadvantages and subordination are emphasized, the nature and consequences of men's advantages get overlooked. In a similar vein, Carbado proposes that heterosexual privilege operates in much the same way in part because white, heterosexual men do not perceive themselves as marked by gender, race, or sexual orientation: "To put the point a little differently, white heterosexual male identity is socially construed to be normative."[32]

Among Carbado's interventions is a list of "heterosexual privileges." The items included in the list are intended to show heterosexuals how homophobia is not merely something that disadvantages gays and lesbians but also something that advantages straight people. Many of the forty-four items on the list can be attributed to the fact that self-identified heterosexuals are a numerical majority of the population; identifying oneself as heterosexual is simply unnecessary because it is the default category. Other items, however, offer insight into why opponents of lesbian and gay marriage fought so hard to maintain their monopoly on marriage and help explain why the procreation argument was enlisted to that end. Many of the items in the list suggest that lesbian and gay marriage may have the potential to destabilize frequently unquestioned assumptions about heterosexuality and heterosexual procreation in particular. Carbado's list is made all the more potent and useful by its juxtaposition of sexual orientation and race. Following are five of his observations about heterosexual privilege that also implicate the procreation argument:

> 5. The children of a heterosexual couple will not have to explain why their parents have different genders—why they have a mummy and a daddy.

Conversely, although the children of a lesbian or gay couple may be called upon to narrate the origins of their families in ways that the children of straight couples would not, unraveling this particular form of privilege raises the question of origins for children of all types of families. In his book *The Kid*, Dan Savage describes an informational meeting for partners seeking to adopt, and one of the striking things he describes is the almost shameful tone with which the straight couples in the group confessed their inability to conceive and produce biological children. Adoption, for them, was a last resort, a final desperate act in an attempt to make a family.[33] While increasing numbers of families rely on adoption and assisted reproductive technologies, and the stigma associated with such practices has diminished considerably, proponents of the procreation argument assumed this form of heterosexual privilege as a way to avoid altering the fictional narrative of the traditional, natural, biological family where reproductive capacity would never need to be questioned, especially by children.

> 19. Child molestation by heterosexuals does not confirm the deviance of heterosexuality (though if the alleged molester is Black, the alleged molestation becomes evidence of the deviance of Black (hetero)sexuality).

I will return to this theme in the following chapter as it is among the most potent and problematic aspects of heterosexual privilege. Although some feminists, most notably Catharine MacKinnon and Andrea Dworkin, have characterized all heterosexual intercourse as rape, on a broader cultural level rape remains a highly contested social, political, and legal problem that is rarely characterized as a heterosexual problem in the same way that cases of child sexual abuse are routinely overlooked when adult males abuse girls but gain wide media attention when the victims are boys.

The procreation argument originates from the premise that dual-gendered marriage must be maintained in order to tether biological fathers to the women they impregnated. Thus, the abortion debate in the United States unfolds at the intersection of how couples become (or avoid becoming) parents (number 5 from Carbado's list) and forms of sexual excess (number 19). Disrupting these forms of heterosexual privilege could, and should, resignify abortion as a medical problem that is not confined to one gender. Just as the problem of rape on college campuses has begun to focus on reeducating young men about sexuality, so too must contraception and abortion be degendered with the reeducation of men.

> 23. Children will be taught in school, explicitly or implicitly, about the naturalness of heterosexuality (they will also be taught to internalize the notion of white normativity).

This particular heterosexual privilege could well be expanded to include many more social institutions; it would be impossible to shield children from information about the heterosexual lifestyle as it is culturally ubiquitous. After the Massachusetts Supreme Court decided *Goodridge*, parents in that state immediately turned to the courts to prevent children from being taught that homosexuality was normal or natural, ideas that were contrary to their Christian beliefs. The parents objected to the fact that their son had been exposed to a children's book entitled *King*

& King, the story of a prince who, by the end of the tale, marries his boyfriend. The parents asked the school district to exempt their children from any discussions involving sexuality, and in a curious capitulation to heterosexual privilege, the court left open the legal question of whether or not discussing homosexuality was, in and of itself, a discussion of sexuality. What is odd about such a question is what it reveals about heterosexuality. If *King & King* can be interpreted to be about sex or sexuality, then so must *Cinderella*, *Snow White*, and much other children's literature. What proponents of the procreation argument hoped to maintain in this moment of heterosexual privilege is the false, unsupportable, yet commonplace belief that heterosexuality is not about sex. This also provided a crucial turning point in the debate: either homo- and heterosexuality are about sex or they are not. Justice Kennedy's opinions for the Supreme Court brought homosexuality out of the sexual domain and cloaked it instead in the mantle of romance.

> 25. Heterosexuals can adopt children without being perceived as selfish and without anyone questioning their motives.

This item is a direct response to the now-discredited canard that because gay and lesbian couples could not reproduce by "natural" means, they would need to recruit future generations of gay and lesbian children through other means. The corollary of this premise—that gays and lesbians did not need marriage because they could not reproduce accidentally—crumbled comically under judicial scrutiny.

> 33. The parents of heterosexuals do not love them "in spite of" their sexual orientation, and parents do not blame themselves for their children's heterosexuality.[34]

Based on the premise that gay and lesbian children are flawed, this item beckons consideration of the place social science research occupied throughout the marriage debate. Volumes of scholarly evidence were presented in courts attesting to the fitness and success of lesbian and gay parents. At the same time that gay and lesbian parents are as likely as straight people to raise children of either sexual orientation, some research suggests that children of lesbians and gays feel less confined by gender norms and are more likely to view their own sexual orientation as more fluid. Operating at the intersection of sexuality and gender, the dissipation of this aspect of heterosexual privilege now operates outside the confines of the family and can be seen across the cultural spectrum.

Proponents of the procreation argument assumed these forms of heterosexual privilege as premises and worried about what forms of resignification would take place if lesbian and gay couples were allowed to marry. The concerns of the dissenting justices, primarily their sincere wish not to hear these cases at all, would have preserved their heterosexual privilege by forcing it to remain out of sight. In moments such as Justice Alito's comment that 40 percent of children are born to unmarried women, we can also see how male privilege is part of the package that the dissents wanted to avoid. As the procreation argument developed and became more elaborate, the pathological excesses, deviance, and damaging potential of sexuality could no longer be associated with homosexuality alone; heterosexuality stood to lose its status as an unmarked category. Those opposed to lesbian and gay marriage would now be expected to keep their prejudices to themselves, a serious compromise of their previous position of privilege.

5

A Union Unlike Any Other

The dissenting opinions examined in the previous chapter worked to preserve heterosexual privilege, particularly of the masculine variety, and lamented the possibility of its waning influence. Looking to the past with reference to Locke, Cooke, and Blackstone, and wishing for different results in both *Windsor* and *Obergefell*, the dissenting justices lament the leveling of social hierarchies they once stood atop. The majority opinions in both cases work very differently in that they invite readers to reconsider what Gayle Rubin called the "charmed inner circle" of marital, reproductive, vanilla, domestic, and heterosexual sex. That inner circle has expanded. Good, state-sanctioned sex remains marital and domestic, but the other terms in her formulation have changed somewhat. If properly marital and domestic, indeed domesticated, gay and lesbian sex may now be considered vanilla too, and the term "reproductive" has given way to what might more accurately be called familial. Justice Kennedy's opinions for the Court majorities in both *Windsor* and *Obergefell* refuted the procreation argument and some of its more pernicious effects.

Windsor

Justice Kennedy's majority opinion in *Windsor* begins with the summary of Edith Windsor and Thea Syper's relationship. After tracing the procedural background of the case and locating its origins in the Defense of Marriage Act, Justice Kennedy turned his attention to the theory of justiciability, addressing the question of whether or not the case was properly before the Court. Rebutting the arguments of the dissenting justices, the majority opinion considers the nonadversarial nature of the case. Despite agreement between the executive branch and Windsor, Justice Kennedy asserts that failing to consider the case on the merits would "undermine the clear dictate of the separation-of-powers principle that when an Act of Congress is alleged to conflict with the Constitution, it is emphatically the province and duty of the judicial department to say what the law is."[1] Insofar as the dissenting justices saw the decision as an improper exercise of judicial power, Justice Kennedy argues that refusing to hear the case would abdicate the Court's responsibility to attend constitutional disputes between the executive and legislative branches.

While the Court's majority and dissenting opinions differ sharply in their theories of justiciability, the cultural shifts signified by the opinion arrive in a discussion of the intent and effect of DOMA. Whereas New York State had acted to identify gays and lesbians as a class and to protect their families, Justice Kennedy observes:

> The Federal Government uses this state-defined class for the opposite purpose—to impose restrictions and disabilities. That result requires this Court now to address whether the resulting injury and indignity is a deprivation of an essential part of the liberty protected by the Fifth Amendment. What the State of New York treats as alike the federal law deems unlike by a law designed to injure the same class the State seeks to protect.

Justice Kennedy's opinion describes DOMA as intentionally designed to harm lesbians and gays: "The avowed purpose and practical effect of the law here in question are to impose a disadvantage, a separate status, and so a stigma upon all who enter into same-sex marriages made lawful by the unquestioned authority of the States." In contrast to Justice Scalia's dissent, he refers specifically to the legislative history of DOMA and to the language of the statute as intentionally interfering with the dignity of lesbian and gay marriages through an expression of moral disapproval of homosexuality. The law was clearly intended, he notes, to identify a subset of marriages that were legally recognized by the states and to make them unequal, to establish that those relationships are unworthy of respect and dignity, and to demean the families that lesbian and gay marriage would otherwise place on par with traditional, heterosexual ones.[2]

This theme of demeaning lesbian and gay relationships, making them unequal, and denying them dignity and respect runs throughout Justice Kennedy's opinion, but it is aimed with special force at the relationship between children and their parents despite the fact that Windsor and

Spyer did not have children. Children and childhood appear in six different passages in the *Windsor* opinion, and while two of those references are included to underscore the fact that family law is primarily the province of the states, the other four seem to have had a different purpose:

> Slowly at first and then in rapid course, the laws of New York came to acknowledge the urgency of this issue for same-sex couples who wanted to affirm their commitment to one another before their children, their family, their friends, and their community.
>
> The differentiation [in marriage laws] demeans the couple, whose moral and sexual choices the Constitution protects, and whose relationship the State has sought to dignify. And it humiliates tens of thousands of children now being raised by same-sex couples. The law in question makes it even more difficult for the children to understand the integrity and closeness of their own family and its concord with other families in their community and in their daily lives.
>
> DOMA also brings financial harm to children of same-sex couples. It raises the cost of health care for families by taxing health benefits provided by employers to their workers' same-sex spouses. And it denies or reduces benefits allowed to families upon the loss of a spouse and parent, benefits that are an integral part of family security.
>
> DOMA instructs all federal officials, and indeed all persons with whom same-sex couples interact, including their own children, that their marriage is less worthy than the marriages of others.[3]

Justice Kennedy's opinion accomplishes a number of things, and not least among his goals is acknowledging the financial harms DOMA caused to families that were denied state recognition. These references to the dignity and value of families—particularly those with children—appear in *Windsor*, and their effect culminates in *Obergefell*: they take gender and its attendant power dynamics out of the law of marriage, but, more important, they also take sex out of the family. Unlike the dissents, the Court here displays no worry about demeaning or diminishing the value of traditional marriage by including lesbian and gay couples. Indeed, the intended effect is exactly the opposite: to grant them recognition and dignity.

Obergefell

Justice Kennedy's opinion in *Obergefell* begins by declaring the importance of marriage. It is "transcendent"; it has "promised nobility and dignity"; it is "sacred" and "greater than just the two persons"; it arises from "the most basic human needs"; and it is "essential to our most profound hopes and aspirations."[4] Just as the dissenting justices anchored their definitions of marriage in ancient texts, Justice Kennedy describes marriage with reference to the writings of Confucius and Cicero: "There are untold references to the beauty of marriage in religious and philosophical texts spanning time, cultures, faiths, as well as in art and literature in all their forms."[5] But, unlike the dissents, he concludes that this ancient history is the beginning of the cases at hand, and "respondents say it should be the end as well," because for those opposed to lesbian and gay marriage, extending marriage rights to them would "demean a timeless institution." This recitation of the enduring value of the "profound commitment" that is marriage precedes Justice Kennedy's description of the plaintiffs in the case. He begins with James Obergefell, whose partner, John Arthur, died of amyotrophic lateral sclerosis. Due to Arthur's medical condition, the two were married in a medical transport plane on the tarmac in Maryland but upon returning to their home in Ohio were forced by the state to remain legal strangers. Next he discusses April DeBoer and Jayne Rowse, codefendants from Michigan, two nurses whose adopted, special-needs children are seen by the state of Michigan as having only one parent. Ijpe DeKoe and Thomas Kostura are discussed third. Justice Kennedy informs readers that DeKoe served in the army and before being deployed to Afghanistan married Kostura. DeKoe served in the army "to preserve the freedom the Constitution protects," but he "must endure a substantial burden" because the state of Tennessee refuses to recognize his marriage as legitimate. With these passages Justice Kennedy not only rebuts the arguments put forth by the dissents but also begins the process of weaving gays and lesbians into the ancient and sacred institution from which they had been previously excluded.

The opinion then turns to a brief history of marriage, one that emphasizes simultaneously its timelessness and the many changes that have taken place throughout history, most notably insofar as the move away from coverture altered the influence of gender. Justice Kennedy links these changes to the historical shifts in how homosexuality was known. Gays and lesbians, he notes, moved from pathology and outlaw status to people whose privacy rights were respected by the Constitution. Unlike the dissenting justices who set aside the temporal disconnect between marriage and homosexuality, these historical sketches are woven together as a fundamental premise of the argument to follow.

Justice Kennedy concludes that lesbian and gay couples may exercise the right to marry and argues that the fundamental right to marriage found in the Constitution applies to gays and lesbians just as it does to straight people. A portion of the opinion is then committed to articulating the four "principles and traditions" he sees at the center of the Court's marital jurisprudence: "A first premise of the Court's relevant precedents is that the right to personal choice regarding marriage is inherent in the concept of individual autonomy." With reference to the holding in *Zablocki* that would have prohibited marriage to people in arrears on their child support obligations, Justice Kennedy asserts that it would be contradictory to recognize a right to privacy with regard to other aspects of family life but to deny individuals a right to enter the relationship that is the foundation of the family and society. He continues, with reference to *Goodridge*, by pointing out that because marriage "fulfills yearnings for security, safe haven, and connection that express our common humanity, civil marriage is an esteemed institution, and the decision whether and whom to marry is among life's momentous acts of self-definition." Justice Kennedy concludes the section by stating that there is "dignity in the bond between two men or two women who seek to marry and in their autonomy to make such profound choices."[6]

The second principle of Justice Kennedy's four expands from the rights of individuals and the relationship choices they may make to the importance and value of forming couples. As he writes, "[T]he right to marry is fundamental because it supports a two-person union unlike any other in its importance to the committed individuals." Drawing upon language from *Griswold*, he describes marriage as a sacred union, an association for a noble purpose. Drawing from *Windsor*, he refers again to the dignity that people may enjoy when they define themselves as part of a couple. With a sentimental flourish he writes that marriage "responds to the universal fear that a lonely person might call out only to find no one there. It offers the hope of companionship and understanding and assurance that while both still live there will be someone to care for the other." He concludes the section with an observation cited to *Lawrence*: "Outlaw to outcast may be a step forward, but it does not achieve the full promise of liberty."[7]

The third principle expands yet again from the couple to include families, those with children in particular, and serves as a direct rebuttal to the procreation argument. Quoting from *Windsor*, marriage allows children to recognize the "integrity and closeness" of their own families and to understand that they are thus not unlike other families in their lives and communities. Excluding lesbian and gay families from marriage not only denies them the financial benefits marriage provides but also is stigmatizing, humiliating, and demeaning to children of lesbian and gay parents. Notably, this section concludes with the observation that a desire, ability, or promise to procreate has never been a prerequisite for marriage in any state. "The constitutional marriage right has many aspects, of which childbearing is only one."[8]

The fourth principle expands beyond the domestic realm to establish marriage and the family as the "keystone of our social order." In this section Justice Kennedy notes that marriage is a public institution that "gives character to our whole civil polity." Additionally, he takes stock of the ways that marriage has evolved over the course of American history, removing requirements of parental consent, racial exclusions, and evolution in the relationship between marriage and gender. At the same time that marriage is here described as the keystone of society, society also pledges to support the couple, offering recognition and benefits to "protect and nourish the union." Additionally, he recognizes that lesbian and gay couples not only are harmed by exclusion from marriage but also are thus "consigned to an instability many opposite-sex couples would deem intolerable in their own lives."[9] Read together, Justice Kennedy's opinions in *Windsor* and *Obergefell* engage with and adjust the meaning and value of marriage in four distinct yet interlocking ways.

The Procreation Argument: From Sex to Child Rearing

When the procreation argument originally appeared in legal discourse, it was simply asserted with little need for discussion or elaboration; gay and lesbian couples could not, by themselves, conceive and bear children and were therefore unqualified to marry. Set against the social reality that lesbian and gay couples were becoming parents and making families, the argument began to receive increased attention and evidence. Litigants began filling in details built from credible social science research and debunking false beliefs and stereotypes. By 2005, lower courts were engaging the argument at length and, in response to a growing body of research, were highlighting the absurdity of maintaining bans on lesbian and gay marriage. Marriage no longer needed to serve as the state's carrot and its stick in order to preserve a sexual social order wherein reluctant fathers were coerced into marriage and pregnant women were made dependent on them in order to excuse the state from any obligations for support. By 2014, when Judge Richard Posner penned his masterful refutation of the argument, it had become laughable. An argument that had been initially posited succinctly as a matter of common sense could not withstand such intensified scrutiny, and heterosexuality started to look like a social problem. Despite repeated and convincing scholarly demonstration that heterosexuality is as much an invented construct as homosexuality, it remained practically bulletproof in its resistance to critique. The movement for marriage equality changed the terms of the debate.

Litigants opposed to lesbian and gay marriage increasingly relied on the procreation argument, and the overall intent of that political strategy was to regulate sex, to channel it exclusively into marriage, and to avoid imposing upon civil society any responsibility for child care, health care, or familial support. Recognizing the problems with this approach, courts and litigants favoring lesbian and gay marriage instead drew an argument that was prospectively focused on the welfare of children. The *Goodridge* court, the first in the nation to grant marriage rights to lesbian and gay couples, was also among the first to recognize that regulating sex was unlikely if not impossible and, by citing the best interests of the child, managed to justify altering the traditional definition of marriage.[10] The majority elaborated the commonsense point by noting that the children of straight couples would not be made more secure when the children of lesbian and gay couples were excluded from marriage. Where the carnal act of sex appeared in the *Goodridge* majority opinion, it was positioned not as a harbinger of chaos but as merely one way that people become parents. Marriage changed from a coercive institution to a consent-based institution, one that promoted stability between partners in order to provide them and their children with state support.

Justice Kennedy's opinions in *Windsor* and *Obergefell* follow this same logical trend, and his treatment of the procreation argument was succinct yet potent. After recognizing that not all married couples reproduce, he writes:

> That is not to say the right to marry is less meaningful for those who do not or cannot have children. An ability, desire, or promise to procreate is not and has not been a prerequisite for a valid marriage in any State. In light of precedent protecting the right of a married couple not to procreate, it cannot be said the Court or the States have conditioned the right to marry on the capacity or commitment to procreate. The constitutional marriage right has many aspects, of which childbearing is only one.[11]

The scant attention Justice Kennedy gives to the procreation argument insofar as it references marriage and sex stands in sharp contrast to the sustained attention he devotes to the relationship between marriage and child rearing. Like the dissenting justices, he also reaches to ancient texts to support his position: "Confucius taught that marriage lies at the foundation of government. This wisdom was echoed centuries later and half a world away by Cicero, who wrote, 'The first bond of society is marriage; next, children; and then the family.'"[12] He invokes children and child rearing on multiple occasions throughout both *Windsor* and *Obergefell*, contesting and adjusting the meaning of marriage as the opposition would have it. Although children were not at issue in *Windsor*, their presence haunted the Court's opinion. The *Obergefell* opinion emphasizes the place of children in families; the importance of providing for children regardless of the sexual orientation of their parents, specifically with reference to the children of the litigants involved in the case; and, perhaps most important, rebuts the absurd assertion that straight couples will be less likely to marry and have children if lesbians and gays are allowed to do so.[13]

Justice Kennedy does two things in the preceding passage. First, he distinguishes the right to marry from the "ability, desire, or promise to procreate." Marriage and procreation are distinct. Second, he emphasizes that the right that protects the married couple's choice *not* to have children is at the heart of the right to privacy. Justice Kennedy references *Griswold* at the outset and, later in the passage, links it to *Lawrence*. If straight couples have a right to privacy that allows them to be legally married and to actively avoid procreation, then there is no logical reason that gay or lesbian couples—those who are childless as well as those who wish to become parents—should not also have access to marriage regardless of their reproductive intentions. The passage narrows the conceptual distance between our understanding of gay and straight couples, and it does so in part by locating children as an important but nonessential ingredient in the marital equation. It is a necessary but somewhat unexpected move for Justice Kennedy to reverse the dynamic relationship between marriage and children. Children are not a necessary and essential element of marriage; marriage is a necessary and essential element of childhood. Franke's rights-bearing couple is entitled to marriage, but children have rights too, and among them is a right to married parents.

Turning marriage away from sex and toward child rearing infuses these opinion with a temporality that is different from that implied by the procreation argument. In response to the assertion that the Court should have stayed out of the marriage debate until it had been argued and decided by the states, Justice Kennedy observes that a similar point was advanced in *Lawrence*. In the years between *Bowers* and *Lawrence*, the law denied gays and lesbians equal dignity and the privacy protections of the Fourteenth Amendment. Although *Lawrence* corrected the Court's error, Justice Kennedy is mindful of the dignitary harms that people endured in the interim, and he observes that the lingering effects of such harm did not vanish immediately when *Lawrence* was decided: "Dignitary wounds cannot always be healed with the stroke of a pen." In *Obergefell* he observed that a ruling against the plaintiff couples would cause the same sort of damage. Obergefell and Arthur would be rendered forever as strangers in the eyes of Ohio law, and the relationship between DeKoe and Kostura would remain unrecognized by the state and nation that DeKoe had served. Perhaps most potently, he makes the point that the children of DeBoer and Rowse would suffer as a result of the state's continued refusal to recognize the marriage of their parents; childhood passes too quickly to hesitate any longer, and "for them and their children the childhood years will pass all too soon."[14] Unlike the dissenting justices in both cases, the Court majority is looking forward rather than backward, and writing lesbian and gay couples into a new temporality, a new version of the future. The Court majority's rejection of the procreation argument places children and their futures above the sexual intimacies of their parents and the regulation of wanton heterosexuality.

Many proponents of the procreation argument were sincerely committed to maintaining the social superiority of heterosexuality. Justice Kennedy rejected that hierarchy:

> The respondents also argue allowing same-sex couples to wed will harm marriage as an institution by leading to fewer opposite-sex marriages. This may occur, the respondents contend, because licensing same-sex marriage severs the connection between natural procreation and marriage. That argument, however, rests on a counterintuitive view of opposite-sex couple's decisionmaking processes regarding marriage and parenthood. Decisions about whether to marry and raise children are based on many personal, romantic, and practical considerations; and it is unrealistic to conclude that an opposite-sex couple would choose not to marry simply because same-sex couples may do so.
>
> The respondents have not shown a foundation for the conclusion that allowing same-sex marriage will cause the harmful outcomes they describe. Indeed, with respect to this asserted basis for excluding same-sex couples from the right to marry, it is appropriate to observe these cases involve only the rights of two consenting adults whose marriages would pose no risk of harm to themselves or third parties.[15]

The assertion that these cases involve "only the rights of two consenting adults" aligns with the Court's privacy jurisprudence and is further evidence of the opinion's elastic uses of children and childhood. Nonetheless, with its rejection of the procreation argument, the Court also refuses to validate the opposition's view of heterosexuality as wanton chaos, with straight marriage providing the solution to a problem.

Lesbians, Gays, and Citizenship

Because *Windsor* revolved around the volatile issue of marriage, that element of the case eclipsed a crucial component of Edith Windsor's claim: because of DOMA, she was being taxed on property that should have been recognized as jointly owned. While she became the face of an important moment in the history of the movement for LGBT rights, we should not forget that because of her victory she was also awarded a tax refund of more than $363,000 plus interest. Two years away from the advance in citizenship signified by *Obergefell*, the move toward economic parity in taxation between gay and straight couples represents a small but important advance in citizenship. The ruling corrected a differential taxation scheme by which Windsor would have been penalized for having a lesbian partner. Justice Kennedy's opinion does more than simply address the unequal taxation scheme: "The particular case at hand concerns the estate tax, but DOMA is more than a simple determination of what should or should not be allowed as an estate tax refund. Among the over 1,000 statutes and numerous federal regulations that DOMA controls are laws pertaining to Social Security, housing, taxes, criminal sanctions, copyright, and veterans' benefits."[16] Justice Kennedy surveys these regulations and strikes down differential treatment by which Windsor would have been penalized; she failed as a citizen and was taxed disproportionately because she is a lesbian.

What is odd about the dissents in *Windsor* is that the Court's champions of neoliberalism, Justices Roberts and Alito, do not mention taxation at all. For them, the possibility of expanding the definition of marriage pushed the economic disparity completely out of view. At the risk of making too much of something that wasn't there, they might have at least included in their dissents a recognition of the fact that Windsor was being unfairly taxed because her spouse was a woman. That they wrote nothing about the subject suggests that their usual emphasis on economics and finance paled in comparison to their concerns with marriage and their own privileged status. More puzzling are Justice Scalia's references to taxation; he makes three. In the first he notes that the United States suffers an injury when it is ordered to issue a tax refund. In the second he worries that striking down DOMA will create confusion among states, asking of couples that move from states that support lesbian and gay marriage to those that do not: "When the couple files their next federal tax return, may it be a joint one?" In the third reference he uses the federal estate tax exemption to illustrate the sort of confusion that DOMA was intended to prevent. DOMA, he insists, was not enacted because of animus toward gays and lesbians; it was simply "stabilizing jurisprudence."[17] Justice Scalia's disingenuous interpretation would subject Windsor to an unfair tax burden, but for him, such a result was preferable to causing administrative confusion or inconvenience for the state, a state that was the suffering victim of a lesbian taxpayer.

Justice Kennedy's fourth principle, discussed earlier, also illustrates a rhetorical strategy intended to weave lesbians and gays into the fullness of American citizenship. In the same manner that his temporal framing of precedents and history brought lesbian and gay couples into the narratives of the future, the citations offered by Justice Kennedy in *Obergefell* show how gays and lesbians have become citizens: homosexuality was decriminalized; gays and lesbians were granted the same right of sexual privacy available to straight people; DOMA fell; lesbian and gay marriage became a national reality.

Marriage at the Vanishing Point

In geometry, parallel lines are always the same distance apart, and they never meet. In linear perspective, however, depth and distance are rendered perceptible in two-dimensional spaces through the illusion of convergence on some distant horizon. Law and culture—often perceived to be geometrically parallel—may be more accurately understood as representations in linear perspective. Sherwin's suggestion that law and culture ultimately converge at the vanishing point in a two-dimensional space invites us to think about what happens when the two intersect; they become indistinct. Coupled with Calavita's observation—that formal law sometimes undermines the very social structures it aims to preserve—this suggests that when law and culture meet on a distant horizon, friction results. For Edelman, reproductive futurism propels us toward this distant, unreachable destination that is always receding from the viewer's gaze, but even as we move toward it, we can see its garish features. Heterosexuality is the unreachable distant point on the horizon; as the preceding chapters have shown, the viewers' eyes catch many intricate designs, patterns, and landmarks as we move across the marital landscape. The formal law of marriage intersected with change and evolution in the ways we know sexuality, gender, and the family, and rather than compromise the sacred cultural value of marriage, formal law was adjusted to accommodate a new reality.

Becoming legally straight brings gay and lesbian people into a system that reinforces many of the structures and privileges previously limited to straights. Much good may come from this, but it is not without risks. We may have arrived at the moment Michael Warner foreshadowed in *The Trouble with Normal*: the "good gays" are getting married, becoming parents, going to church, and serving in the military, while the "bad gays" are disrupting gender norms, having risky sex, eschewing monogamy, and failing to imitate and reaffirm the heteronormative ideal of the neoliberal family.[18] In reality, however, few people—gay or straight—live up to the fullest manifestations of the fantasy ideal because that, in itself, would be too confining at best, but more likely impossible.

As heterosexuality has lost its heuristic monopoly on the organization of sex, reproduction, and the family, its regulatory functions are being relocated. Gayle Rubin's concerns with the ordering of sexuality—policing gender, maintaining hierarchies of sexual value, refusing the possibility that sexual variation may be benign, and reestablishing what she called the "charmed inner circle" of sanctioned sex—have not gone away. In fact, it seems very likely that the forces of regulation are becoming even more extreme and the threats of punishment for transgression more draconian. After the Supreme Court issued its ruling in *Windsor*, gays and lesbians were not the only ones celebrating. Some feminist organizations joined in the celebration, too. Katherine Spillar, executive vice president of the Feminist Majority Foundation and executive editor of *Ms. Magazine*, issued the following statement in response:

> Along with millions of other feminists, Ms. magazine and the Feminist Majority Foundation are celebrating the two U.S. Supreme Court decisions today that declared the Defense of Marriage Act unconstitutional and let stand a lower court decision that California's Proposition 8 is also unconstitutional. . . . Feminists in California fought like hell to defeat Proposition 8 when it came on the ballot in 2008. I joined the board

> of Equality California, along with Feminist Majority Foundation board member Dolores Huerta, to strengthen the connections between the feminist and LGBT communities in the major human rights issue.

Eleanor Smeal, president of the Feminist Majority Foundation, was quoted as follows:

> At last Prop 8 and DOMA are finished. Marriage equality lives in California, the biggest state in the nation. And the federal government must recognize marriage equality in 13 states and the District of Columbia, covering 30% of the nation's population. There is still work to do, but victory is in sight. On the 10th anniversary of *Lawrence v. Texas*, the Court takes another major step towards equality.[19]

That such prominent feminists supported lesbian and gay marriage with such enthusiasm is a sign of change. For many socialist and third-wave feminists in particular, marriage was a primary locus of patriarchal power; thus the change meant many things, including a deepening alliance between the women's and LGBT movements; a re- or degendering of the institution; a civil rights victory for the LGBT movement; a cause for celebration.

Obergefell worked a further significant diminution of the place of gender in marriage law. As Justice Kennedy writes, marriages were once arranged by a couple's parents, "but by the time of the Nation's founding it was understood to be a voluntary contract between a man and a woman." Coverture, however, made the result a single "male-dominated legal entity." He goes on to explain that as women gained legal, political, and property rights, society also began to understand that they have "their own equal dignity," and therefore the law of coverture was abandoned. Such developments were not merely superficial; they affected deep changes in the institution, transforming its structure and altering aspects of it that had been "long viewed by many as essential."[20] Coverture appears again later in the opinion with reference to the changes that took place in the 1970s and 1980s. Despite its erosion, "[o]ne State's law, for example, provided in 1971 that 'the husband is the head of the family and the wife is subject to him; her legal civil existence is merged in the husband, except so far as the law recognizes her separately, either for her own protection, of for her benefit." Responding to such beliefs, the courts began invoking the equal protection clause of the Fourteenth Amendment to invalidate laws that perpetuated sex-based inequality in marriage.[21]

Throughout the marriage debate, scholars have contemplated what might or might not happen should lesbian and gay couples begin getting married. Some have predicted, hoped, or suggested that allowing lesbians and gays to marry would improve and strengthen the institution; others have been less convinced that it would change much of anything; still others see it as the end of civilization. In an extensive critique of feminist perspectives on the marriage debate, Barker argues that, "while there is some debate about what the implications of same-sex marriage could be for the critique at the individual level, at the structural level there is no distinction between same-sex and different-sex marriage."[22] She describes radical feminist critiques of marriage as looking to heterosexuality itself rather than at marriage per se as the site of women's oppression. Kaplan has proposed that lesbian and gay marriage would be a form of civil disobedience that could have the potential to destabilize heterosexist norms, thus bringing gays and lesbians out of the closet and into the public sphere.[23] Warner and Seidman have both expressed the concern that lesbian and gay marriage would have the effect of assimilating "good gays" (i.e., stable, monogamous, reproductive, couples) into a heteronormative model, thereby potentially relegating "bad gays" (i.e., the polyamorous, nonmonogamous, gays and lesbians who preferred a more liberationist model of sexuality or more fluid forms of family formation) to more marginal cultural positions.[24] Polikoff has explained why lesbian and gay marriage will not alter the dynamics of the sex-gender system as we might anticipate.[25] Franke described the potential for loss as follows:

> We had a thick account of stranger sociability, of intimacy, of desire, and of ways in which the political "I" would not presuppose a domestic and domesticated affiliation with a "You," thereby collapsing into a "We." To my ear, the loss of the concept of "me" into a conjugal, domesticated "we" at times echoes a longing for a kind of contemporary coverture, whereby one or both previously individuated subjects are dissolved into a joint legal and economic unit by and through the institution of marriage.[26]

She continues by emphasizing that not everyone advocating for lesbian and gay marriage insists on such a contemporary form of coverture, "but enough of the arguments in this domain emit such an odor that it gives me great pause."[27] Franke is among a number of scholars who have expressed concern about what unique features of gayness and larger aspirations for social justice have gotten lost or overlooked in the drive toward lesbian and gay marriage. Halberstam, who is suspicious of the traditional, teleological narrative, encourages readers to find pleasure in the alternatives, in resistance to the developmental arc described by the dominant narrative. What Halberstam has called the queer art of failure offers a way to find value in life narratives that worked in other, nontraditional, ways.[28] The hopeful, rebellious optimism expressed by these scholars aspires toward a more just and survivable future, and for many that is undoubtedly the outcome the decisions have set in motion. Justice Kennedy's opinions have incorporated lesbian and gay couples into the dominant narratives of success and futurity. But buried beneath the enthusiasm for marriage and the jubilation over success are many of the same problems that have long haunted the LGBT movement, as well as the rights of women, transgender people, young queers, and people with HIV.

In his rejection of the repressive hypothesis, Foucault showed that the Victorian era, erroneously thought to be a time of suppression and silence, would be better described as a moment when discourses about sexuality proliferated and emerged in multiple new locations. Throughout the marriage debate the discourses of heterosexuality have undergone a similar transformation. Tension between the proponents and opponents of the procreation argument, the variations in its uses, coupled with the rhetorical elaboration to which heterosexuality has been subject have not only effectuated changes in the formal law of marriage but also moved the discourses of sexuality to different locations with different objectives and emphases. Among the premises grounding the procreation argument were beliefs about the construction of gender, particularly the preservation of male sexual agency and privilege. Meanwhile, women's sexuality, reproductive choices, and bodily integrity remained targets of increasing regulation. The main premise of the procreation argument assumed that heterosexuality is a messy business. Resistance to lesbian and gay marriage by opponents was not simply about disallowing lesbian and gay marriage. It was also resistance to, and fear of, changes in the system of gender and sexuality, privilege, and regulation. Heterosexuality is thus part of the social script by which people understand and value their own gender identities and situate themselves within a grid of social relationships. It allows people to know how to negotiate the world without having to question what they think they know about others. The advances in LGBT rights and the changes in the law schematized in Justice Kennedy's opinions threatened to destabilize traditional ways of occupying one's ostensibly natural gender. But the changes did not happen exactly as we might have predicted or without side effects.

In the same ways that marriage is mistakenly thought of as a timeless, ahistorical, natural, unchanging institution, proponents of the procreation argument make the same assumptions about gender. When proponents of the procreation argument, including the dissenting justices of the Supreme Court, reach backward through history to ground their arguments in opposition to lesbian and gay marriage, they perpetuate a fiction that should be understood as undermining their own argument. Although it is true that marriage has historically been a male-female institution, its purposes and the social need for it were very different in the time of Locke, Blackstone, Cicero, and Confucius. Inasmuch as each of those writers valued the family as the foundation of society, it is inaccurate and disingenuous to draw from their writings an opposition to other forms of marriage because, at the time they were writing, the homo-hetero distinction did not yet exist as an organizing social script. Justice Kennedy's opinions set aside this artifice and rely upon the ancient works to establish the value of the family as it exists in the present. The family may be the timeless institution at the foundation of the nation, state, and society, but when proponents of the procreation argument worried about imminent chaos, among their primary concerns was maintaining the family as the principal training ground for perpetuating the gender binary. Having lost the argument, however, does not mean that gender, gender training, and our cultural fascination with gender have subsided. In Foucauldian fashion they have, instead, simply relocated.

Focusing attention on children and childhood—a strategy commonly seen among conservative political forces—has not turned out quite as some had planned. Our conception of childhood as a timeless, ahistorical, biological fact overlooks the ways that it is now, and always has been, socially constructed in law and culture. Children are no longer the inevitable and unavoidable result of heterosexual intercourse, and neither are they seen as primarily economic resources for their families. What is more recent, as Foucault, Ariès, and others have shown, is that childhood has become a phase of life when sexual innocence is one of the most, if not *the* most, important markers of health and normalcy. In an earlier era, the time of innocence, education, and socialization that we today associate with childhood was compressed into a much smaller period of an individual's life, if it existed at all, and the privilege of having a childhood was more heavily dependent upon differences in class and race. Children of color and those from lower economic levels often survived under considerably more harsh circumstances than their more affluent counterparts.[29]

At the same time that U.S. courts were refusing to recognize lesbian and gay marriages, they were, with increasing frequency, enforcing the legal and financial obligations of gay and lesbian parents regardless of the genetic, biological, or legal ties they shared with their children. If the procreation argument were focused precisely on the moment of conception, reproductive futurism would have suffered and the marital fantasy associated with it would have been similarly compromised. Working strenuously to sustain the existing system was not just disingenuous, it was potentially damaging to everyone. Parenting and childhood stand as sacred cultural symbols at the center of the marital fantasy. But, as Edelman pointed out, worrying about the rights of some symbolic, figural child may have helped sustain the cultural superiority of heterosexuality, but at the expense of limiting rights and benefits afforded to "real" citizens, "real" children.[30]

When the dissenting justices in *Windsor* and *Obergefell* looked to ancient texts to support their homophobic philosophies, their rhetorical strategy returned readers to a mythical past and found there a static but specious definition of marriage, one that they hoped to resuscitate and bring into the present where it could stand as a legible guide for the future. Justice Kennedy's opinions rely on a different rhetorical strategy, one that can be seen at work in several different places throughout his opinions. Illustratively, when he sets forth the four "traditions and principles" in support of extending marriage rights to lesbian and gay couples, the principles he articulates begin with the individual and expand outward to the couple, to families, and to the nation. His reference to Cicero, unlike that of Justice Roberts, does the same rhetorical work of moving from the individual in the present forward into a future. His treatments both of homosexuality and of gay rights litigation are also framed in this way. Lesbians and gays moved from pathology to outlaw, outlaw to outcast, and now, with *Obergefell*, were brought into a state of equality with their fellow straight citizens. He relies on the same temporal reframing as he traces litigation from *Bowers* to *Lawrence*, from *Baehr* to *Goodridge*, and from *Windsor* to *Obergefell*, where he informs readers that the very real children of April DeBoer and Jayne Rowse have a future that must be attended, now, in the present.[31] In each of these passages Justice Kennedy renders an opinion that draws a new picture of the future, and he is aware of that fact, describing it as a method that "respects our history and learns from it without allowing the past alone to rule the present." In a refutation of the dissents' backward-looking emphasis, Justice Kennedy informs readers that the "nature of injustice is that we may not always see it in our own times. The generations that wrote and ratified the Bill of Rights and the Fourteenth Amendment did not presume to know the extent of freedom in all of its dimensions, and so they entrusted to future generations a charter protecting the right of all persons to enjoy liberty as we learn its meaning."[32] For Justice Kennedy and the other members of the Court majority, the future is now.

Conclusion

Marital Jeremiad

The movement for lesbian and gay marriage has been about more than simply gaining legal benefits. It has also been a movement committed to shedding both the stigma of sexual deviance and the second-class citizenship signified by civil unions and domestic partnerships. Although the Supreme Court's ruling in *Obergefell* worked rhetorically to refute the vestiges of stigma, becoming legally straight was not the end of the story. Heterosexuality remains an elusive and protean object of analysis, and there is still a great deal to learn about how it functions within a system of gender, reproduction, and the family. Jane Ward's recent contributions offer an especially productive advance. She writes:

> [T]he story of heterosexuality in the twenty-first century is, in large part, a story about the hegemony of bio-evolutionary accounts of sexual desire. It is the story of heterosexuals who believe that they know who they really are, and what they can and cannot change about their nature. And, as such, it is also a story about the capacity of heterosexuals to pretend, to explore, to mess around and mess up, to be fluid and flexible—and then to return home to their presumed essence.[1]

Ward's primary interest is heterosexual masculinity, particularly the ways that straight white men narrate, triangulate, obviate, and consummate their desires to have sexual encounters with other straight white men while, at the same time, shoring up their masculine privilege. As Ward and others have observed, the dominant gender/power hierarchy is enabled and strengthened through a series of feints and denials. Halberstam reminds us that forgetfulness jams "the smooth operations of the normal and the ordinary."[2] "De-linking the process of generation from the force of historical process is a kind of queer project," and for

Halberstam "generation" signifies more than just biological reproduction. Queer failure signifies new opportunities to disrupt heterosexual life narratives by which success is measured according to a predetermined teleological yardstick. Turning attention to the comic buddy film *Dude, Where's My Car?,* Halberstam argues that "forgetfulness and stupidity combine to produce an alternative mode of knowing, one that resists the positivism of memory projects and refuses a straight and Oedipal logic for understanding the transmission of ideas."[3] The procreation argument was designed to preserve a heterosexual mode of knowing, one that depended on very specific types of forgetfulness and stupidity in order to appear coherent, at least on the surface. Moreover, its internal inconsistencies and lapses of logic worked, as Ward identifies, to reinforce identity categories, beliefs about the self, and forms of privilege.

The existence of lesbian and gay marriages is unlikely to have a profound effect on our gendered view of the family or disrupt most forms of privilege. Diminishing the centrality of gender and procreation within marriage does not mean that our anxieties about them have been silenced or that they have subsided; quite the contrary. Rather, our anxieties are being amplified in other ways at other locations, and while some of these issues have been around for a long time, others are rather new. In the previous chapters we caught recurring glimpses of two ideas that merit further attention because it seems that they are becoming increasingly prominent features on the horizon of law and culture: gender socialization and the elasticity of childhood. Both ideas shape how we know sexuality; thus it behooves us to move beyond marriage and take a closer look at how they operate elsewhere. What stories do they allow us to tell? What do they invite us to forget? What forms of privilege do they produce and sustain?

Gender socialization is a large and complex set of processes, and a detailed examination would far exceed my objectives for this concluding chapter. Nonetheless, I want to consider the ways that male children are trained to assume their proper roles as sexual agents with all the masculine privilege that that includes, while female children are raised to assume their roles as sexually passive objects and future mothers. The second aspect of the procreation argument, and an equally forceful component of its operation, is the elasticity of childhood. Our conceptions of childhood, particularly insofar as we think of it as a time of innocence and dependency, expand and contract in ways that are sometimes predictable and at other times surprising. Children are selectively permitted agency and control of their bodies and desires when such freedom serves particular social purposes. At other times, adults who should possess such agency and control are infantilized and denied rights and agency. These tendencies are particularly apparent in several legal and cultural locations: in battles over abortion and women's reproductive rights in general, childhood and sexuality, Title IX, bathroom access for transgender people, and religious freedom restoration acts, to name just a few examples. In these other areas of conflict, forgetfulness and stupidity are shaping the legal and cultural landscape of gender in ever-changing ways.

Gender Socialization

We need not look very far to find evidence for the claim that the procreation argument was part of the antigay hope for preserving the family as a gender training ground. After Massachusetts made marriage available to lesbian and gay couples in 2003, worried parents quickly headed to court. In *Parker v. Hurley* (2007), a U.S. District Court dismissed both federal and state claims raised by Christian parents who objected to the presentation of antihomophobic materials in the public schools attended by their sons. The trouble began when Jacob Parker, a kindergarten student, was given a book depicting various kinds of families—single mothers, interracial families, and one family headed by a gay couple—and Joey Wirthlin, a first grader, was read a story entitled *King & King*, the tale of a prince who married another prince. According to the opinion by Judge Wolf:

> Jacob and Joey's parents each have sincerely held religious beliefs that homosexuality is immoral and that marriage is necessarily only a holy union between a man and a woman. They do not wish to have their young children exposed to views that contradict these beliefs and their teaching of them. The Parkers and the Wirthlins allege that the defendants are attempting to "indoctrinate" their children with the belief that homosexuality and same-sex marriages are moral, and to "denigrate" the contrary view that they wish to instill in their children.[4]

The plaintiffs in the case alleged that the school district had violated their federal constitutional rights of privacy, the right to raise their children as they thought proper, and the right to the free exercise of their religion. As with the dissenting opinions from the U.S. Supreme Court examined in chapter 4, the Parkers were troubled by the fact that their antigay animus not only was contradicted in the public sphere but also would have to be expressed in order to be maintained. The privilege of long-standing homophobic silence was being denied them. Their state claims contended that Massachusetts law required the district to give them notice and an opportunity to exempt their children from curricula that involve sexuality.

Judge Wolf, writing for the court, recognized that the parents had other educational alternatives to choose from and reminded the parents that they had no constitutional right to dictate the school district's curriculum. More potently, the court informed the plaintiffs that while the establishment clause of the First Amendment prohibited the state from endorsing religion, local education officials were responsible for promoting civic values. Thus, while the state may not promote a particular religious point of view, it may teach tolerance for diversity in the hopes of promoting civil dialogue among its citizens:

> It is reasonable for public educators to teach elementary school students about individuals with different sexual orientations and about various forms of families, including those with same-sex parents, in an effort to eradicate the effects of past discrimination, to reduce the risk of future discrimination, and, in the process, to reaffirm our nation's constitutional commitment to promoting mutual respect among members of our diverse society.[5]

Like Justice Kennedy's opinion in *Obergefell*, this passage brings gays and lesbians and their families into the public square as legitimate citizens. The religious objections of the plaintiffs are balanced against the needs of society as a whole, and lesbian and gay families are granted a position of equality in public education.

Despite the generally gay-positive tone of the opinion and its holding, Judge Wolf concluded by engaging a question that has long haunted the study of sexuality. As other scholars have observed, homosexuality is often construed as sexual, while the sex inherent in heterosexuality is eclipsed by its life-giving potential.[6] In the final paragraphs of the opinion, Judge Wolf explains why this is so: "[D]efendants contend that the conduct at issue in this case does not 'primarily involve [] human sexual education or human sexuality.'"[7] He goes on to note that the courts of Massachusetts must be given an opportunity to grapple with this question. Inasmuch as the opinion recognized the citizenship of gays and lesbians, and brought their interests, families, and presence into the public square, the question of whether or not the mere mention of a gay relationship qualified as a discussion of sexuality was left open for future courts to decide. As we saw with *Obergefell*, Justice Kennedy ultimately worked to make homosexuality as much about child rearing and futurity as heterosexuality is thought to be, thereby taking the sex out of homosexuality. In *Parker* the question had yet to be answered. Silencing their antigay animus at school put the Parkers and Wirthlins in the position of having to make sure the gender socialization of their sons would be confined to the private space of their homes, and in conflict with what they were learning in the classroom.

During the campaign for California's Proposition 8, pro-gay and antigay groups produced and aired several television commercials intended to influence the voting public. Antigay ads were frequently built around the belief that marriage is a training ground for children's gender socialization.[8] A prominent theme running through these ads emphasized the confusion children would purportedly experience if lesbian and gay marriage were to become legal. Worries expressed included the possibility that children would not understand gay sexual attraction, that gay sex would be taught in schools, and that children would not be able to comprehend human reproduction if gender were not part of the marital equation. The ads conveyed the worried message that it would be impossible to train children to be properly heterosexual adults in a culture that legally recognized lesbian and gay relationships. Pro-gay ads also featured families with children but emphasized the precarious legal circumstances faced by children whose lesbian and gay parents were unable to obtain the protections of marriage.[9] In these ads parents spoke of their inability to protect their families from medical or economic hardship and of the expenses they would have to incur in order to do so. Both types of ads rendered the procreation argument vividly, in two dimensions and in color, taking it out of courtrooms and into the living rooms of the voting public.

As children and childhood were featured more prominently in the antigay advertising, both types of ads set the scene of gender socialization in childhood; what differed was their depiction of the effect Prop 8 would have on children. Antigay ads played on tropes of gender confusion and telegraphed for the viewer a future when human sexuality and reproduction would become more of a chaotic mess than they already were by casting children in the role of innocent victims of a selfish minority. Pro-gay ads also cast children as victims, but in this instance the assault they telegraphed originated with the state's refusal to recognize their parents' relationships. Both sets of ads located childhood as the training ground for gender socialization.

That childhood is the site of all socialization is an inescapable fact of life and not the issue I want to address. I want, instead, to examine the ways that representations of children vary according to gender and to draw connections between them and the cultural manifestations of the procreation argument. I have argued elsewhere that in the current panic about sexting boys and girls are treated very differently.[10] In that article I traced the story of Marissa Miller and her classmates, teenage girls who were threatened with prosecution after boys in their school circulated images of the girls without their consent. The Miller case and others involving child sexuality share a common preoccupation with the different socialization of boys and girls. One of the lessons we should take from these cases is that girls and gay boys are punished for exercising sexual agency, and their identities are made public as a way to reinforce their shame and broadcast that regulatory message more widely. Presumably heterosexual boys, meanwhile, are often depicted as victims or, when they commit transgressions, are dismissed with the old saw that "boys will be boys." Their identities are shielded from view in order to preserve their masculine, heterosexual privilege. The *Miller* and *Stancl* cases make the point with particular force. In *Miller*, the boys who stole and circulated images of Marissa Miller and her girlfriends were not subjected to either punishment or the publication of their identities. The girls, meanwhile, were threatened with fines, drug testing, and the completion of a course designed to teach them about what it means to be a girl in today's society. In the *Stancl* case, Anthony Stancl duped several of his high school classmates into having sex with him through an elaborate, cross-gender social media ruse wherein he baited his classmates by contacting them through fake online profiles wherein he presented himself as a girl. There, the fact that his classmates produced and distributed pornographic images of themselves and subsequently participated in sexual acts with Stancl, was eclipsed by the media's concern with Stancl's gender deviousness. It is especially noteworthy that prosecutors strove to keep the identities of Stancl's classmates confidential in court documents and that their anonymity was maintained by the media despite the fact that they produced and circulated pornographic images of themselves in an attempt to have sex. Stancl, who is currently serving a seventeen-year prison sentence, was depicted in the press as an abuser not because he was an older man inflicting himself on young boys; Stancl and his classmates were all approximately the same age. Stancl came to be seen in the media as the abuser because of his gendered trickery, and his ruse threatened to disrupt the successful gender training of his ostensibly heterosexual classmates. Both *Stancl* and *Miller* reaffirm the findings of others: girls involved in sexting are punished and branded as sluts, while boys are seen as exercising their privilege as masculine sexual subjects.[11] Similar trends can be seen in media coverage of many other cases such as those involving Pennsylvania State University assistant football coach Jerry Sandusky, former Speaker of the House Dennis Hastert, the ever-widening problem in the Catholic Church, and the suicide of Rutgers student Tyler Clementi, to name just a few. Each of these stories shows that we worry more about disrupting the proper gender socialization of boys, particularly the development of their masculine heterosexual privilege and the sense of themselves as sexual agents. Boys being boys may escape punishment as long as their transgressions are framed by a heterosexual life narrative; they will be punished as adult men, however, if they undermine that developmental narrative for other males. Girls, trained as passive sexual objects, are punished when they exercise sexual agency; they become victims, if not also invisible, so long as they remain passive objects within an economy of reproduction.

The procreation argument as it developed in both law and media did little to disrupt this pattern of socialization and, instead, often helped perpetuate it. Evidence for the claim can be seen in the two television spots referenced earlier. In the pro–Prop 8 commercial we see a girl child being confused by lesbian and gay marriage, with the confusion resulting from the child's inability to properly comprehend where babies come from. The segment in opposition to Prop 8 presents viewers with a lesbian couple and their two sons, one of whom laments his diminished social status among his peers because he is the child of homosexual parents. He speaks of being called a "fag" at school, of the second-class status he occupies, and of his own compromised masculinity. Here, the viewer is invited to believe that the problem would be remedied if his parents' Canadian marriage were legally recognized. The preceding chapters contain numerous examples of this tendency, which can be seen at work most forcefully in the predictions of human reproduction becoming chaotic when gender is removed from marriage. Stated another way, the chaos of single motherhood requires us to forget, in an organized manner, just as Justice Alito seemed to have forgotten in *Obergefell*, that women do not become pregnant without some contribution from men. Maintaining male sexual privilege requires scripted forms of denial, feints that allow power to be exercised by keeping it hidden and forgetting that it is there. That the relationship between power and secrecy is productive is not a new insight.[12] What I want to examine instead is how these ways of unknowing are enabled and extended by what I call the elasticity of childhood.

Elastic Childhoods

If asked to define childhood, most people would probably offer something like this: the period of life that begins at birth and ends with the onset of adulthood. Although definitions of adulthood vary across cultures and legal jurisdictions, sexual maturity is among the most common markers in the life narrative signaling readiness for marriage and reproduction. The narrative power of childhood, however, has escaped these boundaries, extending backward, before birth, into the uterus, and even before that into the lives of women who may carry children (or not). Childhood also frequently extends forward into the adulthoods of men whose proper heterosexual development has been compromised by child sexual abuse. The elasticity of childhood thus disempowers and minimizes the agency of women by erasing them from what

Rosalind Petchesky calls the "scene of pregnancy" while it empowers and foregrounds men by extending the damage from childhood sexual encounters into a confessional present.

Petchesky's pathbreaking article "Fetal Images" details with exceptional clarity how women's bodies and agency are eclipsed and made invisible by enlarged and increasingly prominent representations of fetuses. As she observes, sonogram technology has allowed us to humanize and magnify images of fetuses, presenting them as fully formed citizens with rights claims that pit them against the women carrying them. Although some antiabortion statutes are designed to close women's health care facilities through intense scrutiny and regulation of doctors or health care facilities, others depend on the elasticity of childhood to turn developing fetuses into fully formed, rights-bearing citizens. Illustratively, laws used to protect fetal life may take a variety of forms:

> Such legislation includes feticide laws, drug policies, statutes criminalizing maternal conduct, and statutes authorizing the confinement of pregnant women to protect the health of fetuses. In some instances, prosecutors interpret existing laws intended to protect children from physical abuse to apply to fetuses—and thus these applications also fall within the category of fetal protection laws. According to proponents, fetal protection laws are intended to promote the health and safety of fetuses by criminalizing actual or intended harm to the unborn.[13]

Some fetal protection laws target pregnant women and threaten punishment for behavior that may cause harm to a fetus. In other instances crimes against pregnant women by third parties are legally framed as having involved two victims—the woman and the fetus. Other examples include bans on abortion after twenty weeks' gestation under the disputed theory that fetuses feel pain. More recently, the legislature of Utah passed a statute requiring the administration of anesthesia to a woman terminating a pregnancy after twenty weeks on that same disputed theory.[14] Indiana, meanwhile, has passed a law requiring cremation or burial of aborted or miscarried fetuses, and legislators in Oklahoma passed a bill that would subject doctors to criminal penalties and the loss of their medical licenses if they perform abortions; Oklahoma's Governor Fallin vetoed the bill.[15] Nathan Dahm, author of the bill, is quoted in the *New York Times* as saying, "Most people know I am for defending rights. Those rights begin at conception."[16] Apparently, in Mr. Dahm's logic, rights begin at conception and end when the fetus becomes a woman who is capable of conception. In the weeks following the 2016 presidential election, many antichoice legislators excitedly anticipated a conservative new appointee to the U.S. Supreme Court and a new opportunity to challenge *Roe v. Wade*. In order to advance their backward agenda as quickly as possible, draconian new laws have been proposed or passed. In Ohio, for example, the state legislature passed what has come to be known as the "Heartbeat Bill," a law that would prohibit abortion after a heartbeat becomes detectable, meaning, effectively, that most women would be prohibited from having abortions before even knowing they were pregnant. Texas hastened to pass a law that would require funerals and burial or cremation for aborted fetuses.[17]

In a recent challenge to Wisconsin's severely restrictive antiabortion statute, Judge Posner provided another example of childhood elasticity. In that case, Wisconsin, like many other states, enacted a law that not only required abortion providers to have admitting privileges at a nearby hospital but also allowed the father or grandparents of an aborted fetus to file civil suits against a doctor who violated the statute. As Judge Posner observed:

> And we can't forbear to mention the weird private civil remedy for violations: The father, or a grandparent, of the "aborted unborn child" is entitled to obtain damages, including for emotional and psychological distress, if the abortion was performed by a doctor who lacked admitting privileges. Were the law aimed at protecting the mother's health, as the state contends, a violation of the law could harm the fetus's father or grandparent only if the mother were injured physically or psychologically as a result of her abortion doctor's lacking the required admitting privileges. But the statute requires no proof of any injury of any kind to the mother to entitle the father or grandparent to damages upon proof of a violation of the statute.[18]

Additionally, researchers have proposed that women should treat their bodies as though they were already pregnant well in advance of conception, avoiding things such as alcohol or travel to areas of the globe where the Zika virus is prevalent. In these moments, the elasticity of childhood—that is, the childhood of the fetus—begins before birth; indeed, it begins before conception, and with particularly damaging possibilities for women. These aspects of the procreation argument continue to appear with particular force in the ongoing legal battles over women's reproductive health. These types of laws have been promulgated across the United States, and for most of the last twenty years abortion advocates have worried about challenging them before the Supreme Court for fear of losing ground.

Where abortion is at issue, childhood elasticity is usually expansive, stretched toward a breaking point. In *Whole Woman's Health v. Hellerstedt* (2016), the Supreme Court issued a reaffirmation of women's rights to reproductive choice by striking down a Texas statute that effectively closed almost half of that state's clinics under the disingenuous guise of protecting women's health.[19] Rather than ballooning fetal rights at the expense of women's choices, the Court allowed elastic fetal childhoods to snap back to a more sensible size. Given Justice Kennedy's record of caution in previous abortion cases and the death of Justice Scalia, many expected the eight-member Court to deadlock in its ruling. The resultant 5–3 ruling in favor of women's rights surprised many Americans.

The elasticity of childhood operates rather differently when we examine cases involving the sexual abuse of children. Here, my concern is with the gendered differences we see in the news media's treatment of victims. There are, unfortunately, too many examples to choose from. Prominent stories recently in the media emphasizing male victims include the Catholic Church scandals (despite the fact that approximately 20 percent of the victims have been girls) and the story of Anthony Stancl and Jerry Sandusky. Stories involving female victims include those of Jaycee Lee Dugard and the women kidnapped and imprisoned by Ariel Castro. Each of these follows a pattern similar to what we saw earlier with Marissa Miller and Anthony Stancl: when victims are male, their identities are usually kept out of the media; when victims are female, their identities are publicized widely. A second gender disparity seen in these cases involves the gravity and horror of the abuses suffered by the victims. Finally, there is also a differential in the media's treatment of powerful, high-profile abusers; men who abused boys are treated rather differently from men who abused girls.

By now the scandal in the Catholic Church has produced vast volumes of material, including grand jury testimony, news reports, scholarly analyses, and award-winning films. On April 4, 2016, the *New York Times* reported that a Pennsylvania grand Jury had investigated the long history of sexual abuse in the Diocese of Altoona-Johnstown. Featured in that article were the stories told by two of the victims: Maureen Powers and Mark Rozzi. Powers had been abused for two years by the age of twelve, and Rozzi's story of abuse began at the age of thirteen or fourteen. Although both victims came forward and identified themselves voluntarily in order to help bring public attention to the church's cover-up, the grand jury report itself tells the story of thirty-five priests, many of whom had multiple victims. While the structure of the report makes it difficult to determine exactly how many instances of abuse it includes, a rough accounting of the stories it contains confirms the findings of researchers studying the scandal more widely: 83 percent of the victims were male and 17 percent were female. The report identifies each of the priests by name and masks the identities of the victims, describing them only by their age and gender.

Similar patterns can be seen in the cases of Jerry Sandusky and Dennis Hastert. Sandusky, former assistant football coach at Penn State University, was tried and convicted of sexual abuse. Court documents in that case referred to his victims by numbers, and, to date, only one of them, Aaron Fisher, has publicly identified himself. Fisher, whom Sandusky began molesting at the age of fifteen, settled a civil claim against the university for an undisclosed amount of money and in 2012 came out publicly as the person identified in court documents as Victim 1. In an effort to bring attention to the plight of other victims, Fisher published a book entitled *Silent No More*, telling his story and embarking on a speaking tour to draw attention to the problem of child sexual abuse. Although most of Dennis Hastert's victims have also chosen to remain silent and anonymous, one of them, Stephen Reinboldt, has been publicly identified by his sister, Jolene Burdge. In the summer of 2015 Burdge publicly identified her brother as one of Hastert's victims and began telling her story in the mainstream presses.[20] In an interview with ABC News, Burdge explained that she learned of Hastert's crimes when her brother came out to her as gay. As she tells the story, when her brother initially came out, she asked when he had first had a gay sexual experience. The answer was that Reinboldt had begun having sex with Hastert at the age of fifteen. Reinboldt died of AIDS in 1995.

The trauma inflicted upon these male victims must not be denied, but the horrors endured by Jaycee Lee Dugard, Michelle Knight, Amanda Berry, and Gina DeJesus were far more extreme. Dugard, kidnapped at the age of eleven, was held captive in squalor, tortured and raped by a deranged meth addict and convicted sex offender for eighteen years. Impregnated twice, Dugard gave birth in the backyard of her captor's home at the age of thirteen and then again three years later.[21] Parole officers, police, and other state officials remained ignorant of Dugard's nightmare despite more than sixty visits to the home by parole officers and police as well as 911 calls from neighbors. Knight, Berry, and DeJesus endured similar circumstances. Kidnapped by Ariel Castro between 2002 and 2004, the three women, aged twenty-one, sixteen, and fourteen, respectively at the time they were abducted, were kept in captivity, raped, and tortured for between nine and eleven years. During their captivity their abductor impregnated Knight on multiple occasions and in each instance starved and beat her until she miscarried. Berry, also impregnated, gave birth to a daughter in a child's plastic pool with Knight acting as midwife. As in the Dugard case, news reports raised the question of whether the women could have been discovered or rescued had authorities been more attentive.

The stories of Roman Polanski and Samantha Gailey, and Woody Allen and Dylan Farrow are less horrific insofar as they lack the elements of kidnapping and torture, but juxtaposing their stories with those of Dugard, Knight, Berry, and DeJesus illuminates some important variations and similarities. Polanski met Samantha Gailey in 1977 when she was thirteen years old and invited her to participate in a photo shoot, first at the home of Jacqueline Bisset and then at the home of Jack Nicholson. At Nicholson's house the two drank champagne, and Polanski proffered a quaalude broken into three parts. Gailey took part of the pill, and Polanski asked her to undress and get into Nicholson's outdoor Jacuzzi. Gailey testified that when Polanski moved toward her in the water, she feigned an asthma attack and said she needed to go home because she had forgotten to bring her medication. Gailey did not have asthma, and her feigned excuse ultimately served as evidence that she was attempting to avoid Polanski's advances. Polanski instead encouraged Gailey to get out of the Jacuzzi and join him in the swimming pool, which she did. After a few minutes in the pool, Gailey got out to go to the bathroom.

As Jeffrey Toobin reported in the *New Yorker*, Gailey's testimony and Polanski's autobiography begin to diverge at this point in the narrative. According to Gailey, Polanski followed her into the bathroom and told her to go lie down, which she did; she then asked him again to take her home. After responding that he would take her home later, he began kissing her and performing oral sex on her. At her grand jury appearance, Gailey testified that Polanski began performing "cuddliness." When asked to define the term, Gailey replied: "It means he went down on me or he placed his mouth on my vagina." Her testimony also states that she told Polanski repeatedly to stop or to keep away from her and that she did not fight back because they were alone, she had nowhere to go, and she was afraid of him. She also testified that as he was having vaginal intercourse with her, he asked if she was on the Pill. When she told him that she was not, he asked when her last period was. When she said she was not certain, he withdrew from her vagina, pushed her legs up farther, penetrated her anally, and ejaculated.

In his autobiography, Polanski describes the encounter as follows:

> We dried ourselves and each other. She said she was feeling better. Then, very gently, I began to kiss and caress her. After this had gone on for some time, I led her over to the couch. There was no doubt about her experience and lack of inhibition. She spread herself and I entered her. She wasn't unresponsive.[22]

As the two were in the bedroom, Nicholson's girlfriend at the time, Anjelica Huston, arrived and interrupted the scene, at which point Gailey testified that she dressed herself, left the house, and got into Polanski's car. The rape case began that same evening after Polanski showed Gailey's mother and sister the topless pictures. Later that evening, Susan Gailey overheard Samantha telling her boyfriend about the rape; Susan became enraged and called the police. The police took Samantha's statement, then took her to a hospital for examination. Polanski was arrested the following day.

The story of Woody Allen and his daughter Dylan Farrow first made headlines in 1992 when reports of the abuse were filed in court. Investigations launched at that time failed to gain traction in the legal system, and no criminal charges were ever brought against Allen. Officials cited a lack of evidence and the unreliability of the child's testimony. Indeed, much reporting on the case carefully frames the story as one where guilt and innocence may never be known. Subsequently, the story has been reprised in the news media when Allen's celebrity and professional accomplishments attract the attention of the press. In February 2014, when Allen was awarded the Golden Globes Lifetime Achievement Award, Farrow posted the following on her blog. The story was also carried in the *New York Times*:

> What's your favorite Woody Allen movie? Before you answer, you should know: when I was seven years old, Woody Allen took me by the hand and led me into a dim, closet-like attic on the second floor of our house. He told me to lay on my stomach and play with my brother's electric train set. Then he sexually assaulted me. He talked to me while he did it, whispering that I was a good girl, that this was our secret, promising that we'd go to Paris and I'd be a star in his movies. I remember staring at that toy train, focusing on it as it traveled in its circle around the attic. To this day, I find it difficult to look at toy trains.[23]

In May 2016, as Allen was being lauded at Cannes for his most recent film, Farrow's brother Ronan Farrow again brought the story to a wide audience, this time taking to task the news media and Hollywood for overlooking his sister's allegations and failing to even question Allen about the story.

There are, to be sure, significant differences between these stories that explain their varying representations in both law and the media. But for the moment what I want to note are the ways that the elasticity of childhood operates among them. To be clear, none of these stories should be seen as about heterosexuality, homosexuality, or procreation per se. In fact, as Franke observes, these stories are less about sexuality than they are about how sex may serve as a tool of power, victimization, and madness. When we look to the ways that secrecy, the gravity of the trauma, and the status of the abusers operate in these cases, we can see how the elasticity of childhood varies according to the gender of the victims. A documented past of homosexual experiences such as those in the Catholic Church scandals and the Sandusky and Hastert cases threatens to undermine the male sexual agency and privilege afforded to the victims in those cases. As with the Stancl case, the identities of these victims are shielded from public scrutiny in an act of deliberate forgetting that allows the preservation of not only their male sexual privilege but also their ability to control the terms of their predominantly heterosexual life narratives. The elasticity of childhood allows the media to represent the victims—all of whom are now grown men—to be represented in the mainstream media as children, traumatized boys who must not be forced to relive the damaging experiences of their pasts. Dugard, Knight, Berry, DeJesus, Gailey, and Farrow, in contrast, are represented as women, indeed as mothers, adult survivors whose stories are framed by narratives of survival and triumph.

We should pause to question what threshold of trauma and hideousness must be crossed before the news media find such stories newsworthy. While it is possible to read the stories of the male victims as newsworthy because of the large numbers of victims preyed upon in each of the scenarios described here, such quantification alone does not account for the qualitative differences among them. The stories of the male victims are classic examples of how predators groom their victims, deviously seducing them into situations where the crimes committed range from fondling to rape. Such deceptive seduction located within a homosexual narrative frame is, in itself, seen as such a violation that it draws the media's attention. It is, however, so ingrained as a normal part of heterosexuality that the stories of female victims do not rise to the level of newsworthiness absent other far more egregious violations. Sandusky's efforts to groom his victims are monstrous; Allen's and Polanski's efforts to seduce theirs are cloaked with a presumption of innocence. Again, it is the gender of the victims and the elasticity of childhood that help determine which abuses are given headlines and which are not. Traumatized boys are newsworthy; stories of violated girls and women are not. Dorothy Parker once quipped that heterosexuality is not normal, it's just common. We might say the same thing about the victimization of girls: it's not normal, it's just common. So common, in fact, that it easily escapes media attention.

The elasticity of childhood also operates differently along gender lines when the abusers are high-profile celebrities. Because Sandusky and Hastert damaged the heterosexual life narratives of boys, they have been presented in the media as monsters, serial rapists whose actions damned them in the eyes of the press and the public. Polanski and Allen have been subjected to much kinder assessments. In 1977, when the Polanski case began, it garnered attention in the national media, but articles were often short and perfunctory; there were, however, exceptions. The *Washington Post*, for example, ran several stories about the case in its "Style" section, one of which was entitled "In the Land of Dreams and Eternal Youth, Bizarre Events Are Nothing New; Hollywood, Where Craziness Is Nothing New."[24] The article opens with a reference to the upcoming Academy Awards, summarizes the charges against Polanski, and then recants other examples of Hollywood culture run amok, including the arrest of Roscoe (Fatty) Arbuckle, who was acquitted of raping and murdering a young woman at an orgy; Erroll Flynn's acquittal on statutory rape charges involving two young women; producer Walter Wanger's shooting of agent Jennings Lang after learning that Lang was having an affair with his wife. The article then proceeds to report the "chatter in the restaurants and bars" of Hollywood, quoting a waiter who describes the city as "dream land," a place where "[e]verybody thinks they can have anything they want, and they rarely think about the consequences." The piece continues: "In the past year, attention has focused on Hollywood several times in connection with personal tragedies of varying magnitude: Louise Lasser's cocaine possession bust; the unsolved murder of actor Sal Mineo; the suicide of comedian Freddie Prinze." Gossip overheard in the bar at Ports, a restaurant near the old Goldwyn studios, reports that the speaker is "sick and tired—*no, bored*—with all this Polanski chatter." A woman overhearing the statement protests that she is not bored by the chatter, she's offended: "A man's career is at stake. And it's just a typically sexist charge. . . . If some little 13-year old boy came home and told his parents that he had raped Jane Fonda or Liv Ullmann, they'd pat him on the head." Another woman entering the exchange purports to have seen the two together on the night of the incident: "She was the oldest looking 13-year-old chick I ever saw." Friends of Polanski's are also quoted in the article: "No man with sense would try to rape a 13-year-old girl," and "Why does he need rape when he can get a hundred girls?" Returning to the theme of Hollywood lunacy, the article weaves the Polanski incident into a narrative of drugs, sex, debauchery and dreams of stardom but only calls the director's actions into question in the final sentence. "I think I know what it is to be mad," Polanski is reported to have told interviewers, and a sampling of his films is offered in evidence, attached to the adjective "bizarre." The report continues: "He has been called a 'little Napoleon' (he is 5-feet-5). Once asked what drew him to his odd subjects, he said, 'I must be sick.'" While Polanski's legal troubles in the United States continue, so do his career and celebrity status. Media attention to the case arose anew in 2009 after Whoopi Goldberg, host of the television show *The View*, described the case by saying that it was not "rape-rape." As described earlier, the story in 1977 was not one of child sexual abuse but was instead framed within the he-said, she-said narrative of rape. Gailey, now Geimer, responded by writing a memoir of her story that was published in 2013. According to the *Los Angeles Times*, Geimer claims to be more troubled by the press and the media, what she refers to as the "victim industry"—lawyers, judges, and journalists—than by the event itself.[25] The prominence of the rape narrative and Geimer's own attempt to reject her status as a victim are also refusals of childhood elasticity. Hers is not the story of a traumatized child but of a woman whose life has been changed through the standard heterosexual narrative made newsworthy by the celebrity and prominence of one of the players.

In 2014, Dylan Farrow brought renewed attention to her abuse by her father by reposting the story on her blog. When *New York Times* columnist Nicholas Kristof republished it on his blog, he prefaced the publication by asserting that he did so in order to draw attention to the ongoing problem of child sexual abuse. To his credit, Kristof gave voice to a woman who had been otherwise ignored and denied a voice of her own, and he did so by questioning whether Allen should be celebrated with awards given the cloud of doubt surrounding Farrow's allegations. In the preface, he writes, "It's important to note that Woody Allen was never prosecuted in this case and has consistently denied wrongdoing; he deserves the presumption of innocence."[26] On that same date Kristof wrote about the blog post in the *Times* "Sunday Review." In that forum Kristof again reiterates that the story is important because it is about child abuse and not celebrity, but his attention to Allen's place in the narrative indicates that Allen himself must be spared the damaging and libelous possibilities of an overzealous press. He writes:

> Allen's defenders correctly note that he denies the allegations, has never been convicted and should be presumed innocent. There were charges and countercharges. A panel of psychiatrists sided with Allen, a judge more with Dylan and her mother. A Connecticut prosecutor said that there was enough evidence for a criminal case against Allen but that he was dropping criminal proceedings to spare Dylan.[27]

In 2016, the *Times* drew attention to the story again and renewed Dylan Farrow's claims, but that piece, too, preserved the public's ability to doubt her allegations. Allen's case stands apart from Sandusky's or Hastert's in a number of apparent ways, not least of which is the number of possible victims involved. It is also distinguishable from Polanski's due to the fact that in the latter case both parties agreed that sexual contact had taken place. What I want to note, however, is the way that Dylan Farrow's childhood, like Samantha Geimer's, has been denied the elasticity necessary to frame her story as one of child sexual abuse. Dylan Farrow, Ronan Farrow, and Nicholas Kristof have all attempted to reframe the narrative and to keep it in view of the public, but the story is not one of a damaged childhood stretched into a traumatized present; it is a story of a woman revisiting a past history framed by a narrative of doubt and the presumption of innocence.[28] Such representation would not be so noteworthy were it not for the fact that it is so different from the stories told about the victims of Jerry Sandusky or the Catholic Church. There, testimony is offered by grown men who are returned to childhood by the media.

The foregoing section examines the elasticity of childhood as it works in narratives involving children damaged by sexual excesses. But recent developments in the law of Title IX suggest that the same understandings of power and victimization that we see relative to children are being stretched into adulthood. One of the unfortunate trends in the broader understanding of sexuality has always been the manufactured assumption that sex is never without danger. A vast body of scholarship demonstrates that worrying about the proper expression of sexuality has a long history.[29] Recently, however, we have entered an era in which sex is not simply dangerous but is also rarely without a victim. Recent policies enacted in universities across the United States illustrate the point. Lately it has become commonplace for American universities to issue new rules and guidelines designed to regulate sexual behavior among faculty, students, and staff. Such guidelines, like the one instituted at Harvard and emulated in universities across the United States, have garnered a good deal of attention in the media. Such changes, designed to amplify Title IX policies already in place and crafted to prevent sexual harassment and rape on college campuses, establish formulaic scripts that make sex, even consensual sex, an act that always has a victim.

The language of Harvard's newly enacted policy is both expansive and resolute: no member of the Faculty of Arts and Sciences "shall request or accept sexual favors from, or initiate or engage in a romantic or sexual relationship with, any undergraduate student at Harvard College."[30] The exchange of sexual favors for grades, special treatment, promotions, or other institutionally available goods and services has long been prohibited by existing law, and mechanisms for dealing with such problems are well established. Having sexual relationships with students is seen by many as unprofessional, unethical, inappropriate, or in bad taste but, if between consenting adults, not a matter for legal action. Sex and romance are not, however, the same thing, and the inclusion of romance among the newly prohibited activities signals an expanded conception of danger. The new policy takes aim at relationships that may have been desired by the parties involved and potentially pleasurable and also defines institutional power in a way that makes consent impossible between individuals of different social status:

> Although graduate students, teaching fellows, tutors, researchers, and undergraduate course assistants may be less accustomed than Faculty members to thinking of themselves as being in a position of greater authority by virtue of their professional responsibilities, they should recognize that they might be viewed as more powerful than they perceive themselves to be.

The expansive inclusivity of this list guarantees that no two relationships, romantic, consensual, or otherwise, can take place on a field of equal power. The primary target of regulation may be the differential axis of faculty-student relationships, but the expansiveness of the list invites us to recognize multiple other forms of inequality that exist between people of similar social status. The policy not only presumes inequality between any two people but allocates culpability to the one deemed more powerful:

> Even when both parties have consented at the outset to the development of a romantic or sexual relationship between individuals of different University status, it is the person in the position of greater authority who, by virtue of his or her special responsibility will be held accountable for unprofessional behavior.

So, across whichever axes of power a relationship may unfold, someone will be held accountable if things go badly. When sexual harassment, hostile environments, or rape is at issue, such allocation of responsibility may make sense. But the notion that any sexual experience, including romance, always involves an aggressor and a victim is a matter for no small measure of concern. When romances fail, Harvard, and many other universities that have followed suit, now has a ready-made script for allocating blame, responsibility, and punishment. Such scripts are especially useful for universities that are quite rightly accused of promoting a culture of rape on their campuses through their investments in athletics and fraternity culture and by glamorizing the sorts of behaviors that thrive in the toxic atmosphere of masculinity.

In February 2015, Laura Kipnis, professor of radio, television, and film at Northwestern University, ignited a media firestorm after publishing an article about these new Title IX developments in the *Chronicle of Higher Education*. Kipnis opens the piece by revisiting the issue of student-faculty relationships, and although some of her opinions might be debated, the overall concern of the piece is the chilling effect such policies will have on academic freedom as well as the growth and development of young adults. In addition to her suspicions about trigger warnings, Kipnis is also concerned about the ways that Title IX policies may impede students' preparation for life outside academe:

> But what do we expect will become of students, successfully cocooned from uncomfortable feelings, once they leave the sanctuary of academe for the boorish badlands of real life? What becomes of students so committed to

> their own vulnerability, conditioned to imagine they have no agency, and protected from unequal power arrangements in romantic life? I can't help asking, because there's a distressing little fact about the discomfort of vulnerability, which is that it's pretty much a daily experience in the world, and every sentient being has to learn how to somehow negotiate the consequences and fallout, or go through life flummoxed at every turn.[31]

Throughout the article, Kipnis recognizes that sexual assault, harassment, and rape remain serious problems on college campuses, and her concern about the ability of universities to solve the problem is noteworthy. Nonetheless, the backlash against her article seems to have been inspired in part by her resistance to the childhood elasticity signified by these shifts in Title IX policy.

In May 2015, Kipnis published a follow-up to her original article. In the more recent piece she reports that students on her campus staged a protest in response to her original article and that two students had filed Title IX claims against her, claims that were ultimately settled in her favor. Much of the article is devoted to her critique of the byzantine, opaque investigation that ensued. But in a paragraph questioning whether power, consent, romance, and coercion can be effectively managed through Title IX policy changes she asks a strikingly revealing question: "Should eliminating power differences in relationships even be a social goal—wouldn't that risk eliminating heterosexuality itself?"[32] In response to the question we should offer an unqualified Yes! While we are unlikely to eliminate power differences altogether, we can certainly mitigate their more pernicious effects. Eliminating heterosexuality, as unlikely as that seems, would be a step in the right direction. In gender-neutral language, these changes in Title IX policy are also evidence of the ways that everyone is becoming legally straight. The gender neutrality of these new policies makes them applicable to lesbian and gay couples just as readily as to straight ones, and in either scenario, they instantiate power hierarchies that maintain their potency without making clear distinctions along gender lines. They do so now, in part, by turning to the elasticity of childhood to establish new practices for gender socialization. Inasmuch as American universities could do far better at managing the toxic masculinity they regularly promote, worrying about the end of heterosexuality seems misplaced.

As this book goes to press, battles over gender socialization and the elasticity of childhood are spilling onto new—yet familiar—terrain sparked by resistance to the Supreme Court's extension of marriage rights to lesbians and gays. Across the United States, local officials and state legislatures have taken action intended to reestablish heterosexual supremacy. Kim Davis, a clerk in Rowan County, Kentucky, became an overnight celebrity after refusing to issue marriage licenses to lesbian and gay couples. Davis, a four-time bride herself, cited religious objections as her motivation. The ensuing legal wrangling resulted in Davis going to jail and initiated a spate of similar refusals across the country. Rushing to protect the waning heterosexual privileges of people whose objections were purportedly grounded in religious belief, state legislatures turned to the Religious Freedom Restoration Act in an attempt to undermine the Court's ruling in *Obergefell*. Introduced in at least ten states, some of the proposed statutes failed to gain sufficient legislative support, others were vetoed by governors, but those proposed in North Carolina and Mississippi were enacted into law.

North Carolina's law was hastily introduced into the state legislature after the city of Charlotte enacted an antidiscrimination ordinance protecting gay, lesbian, and transgender people from discrimination. The state bill, known as HB2, prohibits local municipalities from enacting antidiscrimination laws, raises the minimum wage, and specifically prohibits people from using public bathroom facilities that do not match their gender as determined at birth. According to the *New York Times*, Republican legislators "stressed that the bill was passed not just to protect women and children from unwanted and potentially dangerous intrusions by biological males, but also to clarify legislative authority."[33] Mississippi's law, described by Samantha Allen of the *Daily Beast*, "would take the state back to the Stone Age."[34] Among the statute's most problematic passages is this:

> The state government shall not take any discriminatory action against a person wholly or partially on the basis that the person establishes sex-specific standards or policies concerning employee or student dress or grooming, or concerning access to restrooms, spas, baths, showers, dressing rooms, locker rooms, or other intimate facilities or settings, based upon or in a manner consistent with a sincerely held religious belief or moral conviction described in Section 3 of this act.[35]

Among the many problematic aspects of the law are the possibilities that it would allow medical personnel to refuse treatment related to sex reassignment surgery or gender dysphoria, including psychological counseling. It would also grant therapists, counselors, and fertility doctors the right to refuse to treat gay or lesbian individuals or couples.

Backlash came swiftly. Several musicians canceled performances in the state, numerous businesses announced boycotts, PayPal and the porn site xHamster withdrew services, and Cyndi Lauper announced that although she would not cancel an upcoming performance, she would donate all proceeds to LGBT groups fighting the statute. The Obama administration also responded to these new statutes quickly and decisively. The Civil Rights Division of the U.S. Department of Justice informed North Carolina that its new law violated federal civil rights statutes and asked the state to forgo implementation or enforcement. In response, North Carolina sued the Department of Justice. Attorney General Loretta Lynch announced the suit in a press conference and, as part of her remarks, offered a passionate defense of the rights of trans people, depicting them as part of the nation's inexorable march toward greater inclusivity and fairness.

Not surprisingly, North Carolina's assault on the trans community quickly became a subject for discussion among presidential hopefuls in the 2016 election. Donald Trump weighed in by saying that the law was unnecessary and invited transgender celebrity Caitlyn Jenner to use whatever restroom she was comfortable with in Trump Tower. The fundamentalist Ted Cruz, who had not yet dropped out of the presidential race, issued a statement in support of the state and took the opportunity to criticize his opponent. Like many other supporters of the law, Cruz immediately invoked the danger to childhood and gender as the truly problematic elements of the law: "Donald Trump is no different from politically correct leftist elites. Today, he joined them in calling for grown men to be allowed to use little girls' public restrooms. As the dad of young daughters, I dread what this will mean for our daughters—and for our sisters and our wives. It is a reckless policy that will endanger our loved ones."[36] Also in response to the controversy, the retail chain Target announced that its customers and employees were welcome to use whichever restroom they felt most comfortable using. Subsequently, a YouTube video of a woman carrying a Bible and storming through a Target store denouncing the policy went viral.[37]

The advent of lesbian and gay marriage will make life a little better for millions of people in the United States. People will enjoy the benefits and happily commit themselves to its obligations. And, like straight couples, lesbian and gay marriages will fall apart; gay divorce is already a growing market. People will get divorced, some amicably and some with wounds and acrimony, and that is one of the most important things about having the right to get married. As *Windsor* and *Obergefell* both make clear, the right to get married is most important when relationships end, when couples divorce or spouses die; when child custody must be determined, estates divided, and taxes paid. Despite all the enthusiastic romanticism that our culture invests in the act of getting married—having a wedding—and for all the heady rituals surrounding that moment, the legal dimensions of marriage are most potent when it is all over. A recent article in the *New York Times* entitled "Why You Will Marry the Wrong Person" says all of the things that no one wants to hear about the reality of the marital fantasy, that is, it's just a fantasy, one that cannot possibly be fulfilled. The author proposes, instead, that we should take a more pessimistic view of marriage:

> A philosophy of pessimism offers a solution to a lot of distress and agitation around marriage. It might sound odd, but pessimism relieves the excessive imaginative pressure that our romantic culture places upon marriage. The failure of one particular partner to save us from our grief and melancholy is not an argument against that person and no sign that a union deserves to fail or be upgraded.[38]

In short, marriages would be a lot happier all around if we lowered our expectations, if the marital fantasy and our unrealistic expectations about the future were tempered with a dose of practicality and realism.

It is impossible to predict in advance how the performative speech act of saying "I do" will resonate in or change the dominant culture, but as Eve Sedgwick once observed, such power effects can be unusually propulsive, like wearing flippers in a swimming pool.[39] A married, straight woman I know was looking to buy a home a few years ago in one of the most expensive cities in the world. One afternoon, while she was working, her realtor called to tell her that she and the seller were only $50,000 apart on their negotiated price. The realtor crooned, "Just think of how wonderful it will be to sit on that balcony, looking out at that view, having your coffee in the morning." The reply to the realtor was probably unexpected. "Listen," she said. "My husband and I are very practical people. We got married because it got us a discount on our car insurance. What I will think every morning on that balcony with my coffee is, 'This cost me $50,000.' Now bring the price down or look elsewhere. And don't call me with any more of this sentimental bullshit." Love, commitment, and practicality are not the same thing as sentimental bullshit, something in which our culture is seemingly awash. We have the vocabulary to speak about marriage in practical terms that are devoid of sentimentality, but we usually refuse to do it. As this book goes to press, I have recently had a wedding of my own. I married a man I have been involved with for more than nine years. And although we, too, got married for practical reasons, such practicality does not mean that there is not also a deep emotional commitment between us, just as is the case with the couple in the story just described. What I found unsettling as our wedding plans advanced was the extent to which I felt invaded by the assumptions and expectations of those around us. People kept excitedly asking me questions that I found baffling: "Are you having a big wedding?" "Are you planning to have children?" "Will you buy a house and move to the suburbs?" "Will you be monogamous?" My answers to these questions ranged from an unqualified "No" to "That is really none of your business." But what they signify is an inability to think of marriage as something *less* than the overdetermined romantic fantasy it represents, and my point is this: marriage is now, and always has been, two things simultaneously. It is a package of legal rights, state entitlements, and benefits, on the one hand, and a floral, lacy, hard-to-maintain fantasy, on the other. It is both law and culture bumping against each other at the vanishing point. Many lesbian and gay couples are now enjoying the fantasy as well as the legal benefits that come with marriage, and that is great. But in the long run what we will probably see is that life, marriage, parenting, and the whole of the marital fantasy will be much the same thing for lesbian and gay couples as it is for straight ones. All the cultural baggage and anxiety associated with the procreation argument, all its flaws and absurdity, will ultimately be as applicable to lesbian and gay couples as it has been for straight ones, with all the chaotic, messy uncertainty that that implies. And that is just fine. That's life.

NOTES

INTRODUCTION

1 Matt Douglas, "The Past, Present and Future of the Wedding Industry," *Huffington Post*, February 24, 2016, www.huffingtonpost.com.
2 Tim Henderson, "For Many Millennials, Marriage Can Wait," *Stateline*, December 20, 2016, Pew Charitable Trusts, www.pewtrusts.org.
3 Claire Cain Miller, "The Divorce Surge Is Over, but the Myth Lives On," *New York Times*, December 2, 2014, www.nytimes.com.
4 See *Bowers v. Hardwick*, 478 U.S. 186 (1986).
5 Pew Charitable Trusts, "Changing Attitudes on Gay Marriage: Public Opinion on Same-Sex Marriage," May 12, 2016. Summaries of these data can be found at www.pewforum.org.
6 Emily S. Rueb, "Is the Recent Spike in Marriages a Trump Bump?," *New York Times*, December 29, 2016, www.nytimes.com.
7 Hanne Blank, *Straight: The Surprisingly Short History of Heterosexuality* (Boston: Beacon Press, 2012).

CHAPTER 1. THE END OF HETEROSEXUALITY?

1 A note on terminology: First, inasmuch as I appreciate the thoughtful extension of this acronym to include queers, questioning, two-spirit people, intersex people, allies, etc., much of the historical material included in this book predates changes in the aspirational movement that such expansion signifies. Consequently, I will use "LGBT" throughout the book when referring to the social movement behind this litigation. Second, although many court decisions and media materials quoted herein use the terms "same-sex marriage" and "opposite-sex marriage," such usage risks reinforcing the false belief that gender is rigidly binary. Because marriages between gay men and lesbians were the focus debate, I will use the terms "lesbian and gay marriage" or "straight marriage" to differentiate as necessary.
2 The Editorial Board, "A Profound Ruling Delivers Justice on Gay Marriage," *New York Times*, June 26, 2015, www.nytimes.com.
3 Rachel K. Jones, Lawrence B. Finer, and Susheela Singh, "Characteristics of U.S. Abortion Patients, 2008, May 2010 Report"; the report can be accessed at www.guttmacher.org.
4 Lauren Sandler, "The Mother Majority: Women with Children Have More Abortions Than Anyone Else, and by an Increasingly Wide Margin. So Why Is the Topic Taboo?," *Slate*, October 17, 2011, www.slate.com.

5 Katherine Franke, "Constructing Heterosexuality: Putting Sex to Work," 75 *Denver University Law Review* 1139 (1998), 1140; Michel Foucault, *The History of Sexuality: An Introduction, Volume I* (New York: Vintage Books, 1978), 103.
6 Adrienne Rich, "Compulsory Heterosexuality and Lesbian Existence," in *Powers of Desire: The Politics of Sexuality*, ed. Ann Snitow, Christine Stansell, and Sharon Thompson (New York: Monthly Review Press, 1980).
7 Jonathan Ned Katz, *The Invention of Heterosexuality* (Chicago: University of Chicago Press, 1995), 13.
8 Ibid.
9 Ibid., 28, 182.
10 See, e.g., Katz, *The Invention of Heterosexuality*; Steven Seidman, *The Social Construction of Sexuality* (New York: Norton, 2003).
11 John Gagnon and William Simon, *Sexual Conduct: The Social Sources of Human Sexuality* (Chicago: Aldine, 2005), 4.
12 For a useful discussion of how different trends of feminist thinking have influenced these debates, see Nicola Barker, *Not the Marrying Kind: A Feminist Critique of Same-Sex Marriage* (New York: Palgrave Macmillan, 2013).
13 Rich, "Compulsory Heterosexuality and Lesbian Existence," 178.
14 Monique Wittig, *The Straight Mind and Other Essays* (Boston: Beacon Press, 1992), 32.
15 Seidman, *The Social Construction of Sexuality*, 105.
16 Gayle Rubin, "Thinking Sex: Notes for a Radical Theory of the Politics of Gender," in *The Lesbian and Gay Studies Reader,* ed. Henry Abelove, Michèle Aina Barale, and David M. Halperin (New York: Routledge, 1984), 104–110.
17 Ibid., 108.
18 Martha C. Nussbaum, *From Disgust to Humanity: Sexual Orientation and Constitutional Law* (Oxford: Oxford University Press, 2010), 1.
19 Laud Humphreys, *Tearoom Trade: Impersonal Sex in Public Places* (Chicago: Aldine, 1973).
20 John D'Emilio and Estelle Freedman, *Intimate Matters: A History of Sexuality in America* (Chicago: University of Chicago Press, 1988).
21 Mary Bernstein and Verta Taylor, *The Marrying Kind? Debating Same-Sex Marriage within the Lesbian and Gay Movement* (Minneapolis: University of Minnesota Press, 2013); Mary Bernstein and Renate Reimann, *Queer Families, Queer Politics: Challenging Culture and the State* (New York: Columbia University Press, 2001); Kath Weston, *Families We Choose: Lesbians, Gays, Kinship* (New York: Columbia University Press, 1991); Evan Wolfson, *Why Marriage Matters: America, Equality, and Gay People's Right to Marry* (New York: Simon and Schuster, 2004).
22 Dennis Altman, *The Homosexualization of America* (New York: Beacon Press, 1983).
23 John D'Emilio, "Capitalism and Gay Identity," in *Powers of Desire: The Politics of Sexuality*, ed. Ann Snitow, Christine Stansell, and Sharon Thompson (New York: Monthly Review Press, 1980), 109–110.

24 Jasbir Puar, *Terrorist Assemblages: Homonationalism in Queer Times* (Durham, NC: Duke University Press, 2007).

25 See, e.g., Michael Cobb, *God Hates Fags: The Rhetorics of Religious Violence* (New York: New York University Press, 2006); Arnaldo Cruz-Malavé and Martin F. Manalansan IV, *Queer Globalizations: Citizenship and the Afterlife of Colonialism* (New York: New York University Press, 2002); J. Jack Halberstam, *In a Queer Time and Place: Transgender Bodies, Subcultural Lives* (New York: New York University Press, 2005); Eithne Luibhéid and Lionel Cantú Jr., eds., *Queer Migrations: Sexuality, U.S. Citizenship, and Border Crossings* (Minneapolis: University of Minnesota Press, 2005)

26 See, e.g., Barker, *Not the Marrying Kind*; Cheshire Calhoun, *Feminism, the Family, and the Politics of the Closet: Lesbian and Gay Displacement* (Oxford: Oxford University Press, 2000); Paula Ettelbrick, "Since When Is Marriage a Path to Liberation?," *Out/Look* 6, no. 9 (1989); Paula Ettelbrick, "One Size Does Not Fit All," 64 *Albany Law Rev.* 905 (1996); Michael Warner, *The Trouble with Normal: Sex, Politics, and the Ethics of Queer Life* (New York: Free Press, 1999).

27 Lee Edelman, *No Future: Queer Theory and the Death Drive* (Durham, NC: Duke University Press, 2004).

28 Philippe Ariès, *Centuries of Childhood: A Social History of Family Life* (New York: Vintage Books, 1965); Foucault, *History of Sexuality*.

29 Peter Hegarty, *Gentlemen's Disagreement: Alfred Kinsey, Lewis Terman, and the Sexual Politics of Smart Men* (Chicago: University of Chicago Press, 2013).

30 Kathryn Bond Stockton, *The Queer Child, or Growing Sideways in the Twentieth Century* (Durham, NC: Duke University Press, 2009); Judith Halberstam, *The Queer Art of Failure* (Durham, NC: Duke University Press, 2011).

31 Amy Adler, "The Perverse Law of Child Pornography," 101 *Columbia Law Review* 209 (2001); see also Amy Adler, "Inverting the First Amendment," 149 *University of Pennsylvania Law Review* 921 (2001).

32 Parker Rossman, "Literature on Pederasty," 9 *Journal of Sex Research* 4 (1973), 312.

33 Bruce Rind, Philip Tromovich, and Robert Bauserman, "A Meta-analytic Examination of Assumed Properties of Child Sexual Abuse Using College Samples," 124 *Psychological Bulletin* 1 (1998), 46.

34 Erica Goode, "Study on Child Sex Abuse Provokes a Political Furor," *New York Times*, June 13, 1999, sec. 11, col. 5, 33.

35 Carol Tavris, "Uproar over Sexual Abuse Muddies the Waters: Suppressing Credible but Unpopular Scientific Findings Won't Reduce the Number of Incidents," *Los Angeles Times*, July 19, 1999, B5.

36 Bruce Rind, "Gay and Bisexual Adolescent Boys' Sexual Experiences with Men: An Empirical Examination of Psychological Correlates in a Nonclinical Sample, 30 *Archives of Sexual Behavior* 3 (2001), 359.

37 Catharine A. MacKinnon, "Feminism, Marxism, Method, and the State: Toward Feminist Jurisprudence," 8, no. 4 *Signs* (1983), 635–658.

38 Kevin Ohi, "Molestation 101: Child Abuse, Homophobia and *The Boys of St. Vincent*," 6 *GLQ* 2 (2000), 196.

39 Jon Davies, "Imagining Intergenerationality: Representation and Rhetoric in the Pedophile Movie," 13 *GLQ* 2–3 (2007), 378.

40 Susan Bandes, "The Lessons of *Capturing the Friedmans*: Moral Panic, Institutional Denial, and Due Process," 3 *Law, Culture, and the Humanities* 2 (2006); Ohi, "Molestation 101," 198.

41 James Kincaid, *Erotic Innocence: The Culture of Child Molesting* (Durham, NC: Duke University Press, 1998); Stockton, *The Queer Child*.

42 Davies, "Imagining Intergenerationality," 380.

43 Rosalind Pollack Petchesky, "Fetal Images: The Power of Visual Culture in the Politics of Reproduction," 13 *Feminist Studies* 2 (1987), 285.

44 Ibid., 287.

45 *Whole Woman's Health v. Hellerstedt*, 579 US ____ (2016); the GOP Platform can be found at www.platform.gop.

46 William Eskridge, "Body Politics: Lawrence v. Texas and the Constitution of Disgust and Contagion," 57 *Florida Law Review* 1011 (2005), 1012, citations omitted.

47 Ibid., 1018, 1024.

48 See, e.g., Ann Burlein, *Lift High the Cross: Where White Supremacy and the Christian Right Converge* (Durham, NC: Duke University Press, 2002); Didi Herman, *The Anti-gay Agenda: Orthodox Vision and the Christian Right* (Chicago: University of Chicago Press, 1997); Hegarty, *Gentlemen's Disagreement*.

49 Richard Sherwin, *When Law Goes Pop: The Vanishing Line between Law and Popular Culture* (Chicago: University of Chicago Press, 2000).

50 See, e.g., Peter Brooks and Paul Gewirtz, eds., *Law's Stories: Narrative and Rhetoric in the Law* (New Haven, CT: Yale University Press, 1998); Austin Sarat and Thomas R. Kearns, eds., *Law in the Domains of Culture* (Ann Arbor: University of Michigan Press, 1998); Austin Sarat, Lawrence Douglas, and Martha Merrill Umphrey, *Law on the Screen* (Palo Alto, CA: Stanford University Press, 2005).

51 Austin Sarat and Jonathan Simon, eds., *Cultural Analysis, Cultural Studies, and the Law: Moving beyond Legal Realism* (Durham, NC: Duke University Press, 2003), 2.

52 Naomi Mezey, "Law as Culture," in *Cultural Analysis, Cultural Studies, and The Law: Moving beyond Legal Realism*, ed. Austin Sarat and Jonathan Simon (Durham, NC: Duke University Press, 2003), 60.

53 See, e.g., Patricia Ewick and Susan Silbey, *The Common Place of Law: Stories from Everyday Life* (Chicago: University of Chicago Press, 1998); Carol Greenhouse, *Praying for Justice: Faith, Order, and Community in an American Town* (Ithaca, NY: Cornell University Press, 1986); Jonathan Simon, "Ideological Effects of Actuarial Practices," 22 *Law & Society Review* (1998); Barbara Yngvesson, "Negotiating Motherhood: Identity and Difference in 'Open' Adoptions," 31 *Law & Society Review* (1988).

54 Kitty Calavita, "Blue Jeans, Rape and the 'Deconstitutive' Power of Law," 35 *Law & Society Review* (2001), 110.

55 Carole Pateman, *The Sexual Contract* (Stanford, CA: Stanford University Press, 1988).

56 Jane Ward, *Not Gay: Sex between Straight White Men* (New York: New York University Press, 2015); Michael Kimmel, *Guyland: The Perilous World Where Boys Become Men* (New York: HarperCollins, 2008).

57 See, e.g., Richard Delgado, "Storytelling for Oppositionists and Others: A Plea for Narrative," 87 *Michigan Law Review* 2411 (1989); Ian Haney-López, *White by Law: The Legal Construction of Race* (New York: New York University Press, 1996).

58 Kimberlé Crenshaw, "Demarginalizing the Intersection of Race and Sex: A Black Feminist Critique of Antidiscrimination Doctrine, Feminist Thought, and Antiracist Politics," *University of Chicago Legal Forum*, vol. 1, issue 1, article 8.

59 Lisa Duggan, *The Twilight of Equality?: Neoliberalism, Cultural Politics and the Attack on Democracy* (Boston: Beacon Press, 2003); Puar, *Terrorist Assemblages*.

CHAPTER 2. OLD AS THE BOOK OF GENESIS

1 *Baker v. Nelson*, 291 Minn. 310 (1971), 312.

2 John D'Emilio, *Sexual Politics, Sexual Communities: The Making of a Homosexual Minority in the United States, 1940–1970* (Chicago: University of Chicago Press, 1983).

3 See Jonathan Goldberg-Hiller, *The Limits to Union: Same-Sex Marriage and the Politics of Civil Rights* (Ann Arbor: University of Michigan Press, 2002).

4 See Kimberly Richman, "(When) Are Rights Wrong? Rights Discourses and Indeterminacy in Gay and Lesbian Parents' Custody Cases," 30 *Law & Social Inquiry* 137 (2005); Mary Lyndon Shanley, *Making Babies, Making Families: What Matters Most in an Age of Reproductive Technologies, Surrogacy, Adoption, and Same-Sex and Unwed Parents* (Boston: Beacon Press, 2001); Judith Stacey and Timothy Biblarz, "(How) Does the Sexual Orientation of Parents Matter?," 66 *American Sociological Review* 159 (2001).

5 *Loving v. Virginia*, 388 U.S. 1 (1967); *Zablocki v. Redhail*, 434 U.S. 374 (1978); *Turner v. Safley*, 482 U.S. 78 (1987).

6 Herma Hill Kay, "Same-Sex Divorce in the Conflict of Laws," 15 *Kings College Law Journal* 63 (2004).

7 For useful discussions of changing narratives and schemas, see Richard Delgado, "Storytelling for Oppositionists and Others: A Plea for Narrative," 84 *Michigan Law Review* 2411 (1989); Patricia Ewick and Susan Silbey, *The Common Place of Law: Stories from Everyday Life* (Chicago: University of Chicago Press, 1998).

8 Judith Butler, "Is Kinship Always Already Heterosexual?," in *Left Liberalism/Left Critique*, ed. Wendy Brown and Janet Halley (Durham, NC: Duke University Press, 2002), 232.

9 For insightful discussions of these changes, see Kathleen Hull, "The Cultural Power of Law and the Cultural Enactment of Legality: The Case of Same-Sex Marriage," 28 *Law & Social Inquiry* 629 (2003); Ellen Lewin, *Recognizing Ourselves:*

Ceremonies of Lesbian and Gay Commitment (New York: Columbia University Press, 1998).

10 Justice Kennedy's opinion makes this disavowal allusively at 567: "This, as a general rule, should counsel against attempts by the State, or a court, to define the meaning of the relationship or to set its boundaries absent injury to a person or abuse of an institution the law protects," and specifically at 578, "*Lawrence* does not involve whether the government must give formal recognition to any relationship that homosexual persons seek to enter."

11 *Standhardt v. Superior Court of Arizona*, 206 Arizona 276 (2005), 283.

12 Ibid., 281, 283.

13 Ibid., 286, citations omitted.

14 Ibid., 287.

15 Ibid., 287–288.

16 Ibid., 288.

17 *Goodridge v. Dept. of Public Health*, 440 Mass. 309 (2003), 367.

18 Ibid., 371.

19 Ibid., 381.

20 Ibid., 382.

21 Ibid.

22 Ibid.

23 Ibid., 388–389.

24 *Morrison v. Sadler*, 821 N.E. 2d 15 (2005), 24–27.

25 Ibid., 26.

26 Ibid., 30.

27 Ibid., 27.

28 Maggie Gallagher, "(How) Will Gay Marriage Weaken Marriage as a Social Institution: A Reply to Andrew Koppelman," 2 *University of St. Thomas Law Journal* 33 (2004), in *Standhardt*, 286–288. For other perspectives on this debate particularly linking marriage to parenting, see Carlos Ball and Janice Farrell Pea, "Warring with Wardle: Morality, Social Science, and Gay and Lesbian Parents," 1998 *University of Illinois Law Review* 253 (1998); Jeffery J. Ventrella, "Square Circles?!! Restoring Rationality to the Same-Sex 'Marriage' Debate," 32 *Hastings Constitutional Law Quarterly* 681 (2004/2005); Lynn Wardle, "Symposium: Tyranny, Federalism, and the Federal Marriage Amendment," 17 *Yale Journal of Law and Feminism* 221 (2005).

29 *Singer v. Hara*, 11 Wn. App. 247 (1974), 264.

30 It should also be noted that the concurrence in *Morrison* was troubled by the explicit link drawn between procreation, sex, and marriage, suggesting that such "laser-like focus" was likely a sign of discriminatory intent (37).

31 *Seymour v. Holcomb*, 7 Misc. 3d 530 (2005); *Lewis v. Harris*, 378 N.J. Super 169 (2005); *Hernandez v. Robles*, 2006 N.Y. Lexis 1836 (2006); *Samuels v. New York State Dep't of Health*, N.Y. Slip Op. 1213 (2006).

32 *Samuels*, 26.

33 This argument appears throughout the majority opinion, where, once again, marriage is depicted as "old as the book of Genesis," with reference to the Mormon practice of polygamy, and in more abstract references to faith and religion. It should be remembered, however, that a number of religious congregations were happy to solemnize the unions of lesbian and gay couples. See *People v. Greenleaf*, 780 N.Y.S. 2d 899 (2004).

34 *Lewis v. Harris*, 195.

35 Ibid.

36 Ibid., 198.

37 See, Gallagher, "(How) Will Gay Marriage Weaken Marriage as a Social Institution"; Didi Herman, *The Anti-gay Agenda: Orthodox Vision and the Christian Right* (Chicago: University of Chicago Press, 1997), esp. chap. 3; Douglas Kmiec, "The Procreative Argument for Proscribing Same-Sex Marriage," 32 *Hastings Constitutional Law Quarterly* 653 (2004/2005).

38 *Hernandez II*, 360.

39 Ibid., 372.

40 For a fuller elaboration of this argument, see Jonathan Goldberg-Hiller and Neal Milner, "Rights as Excess: Understanding the Politics of Special Rights," 28 *Law & Social Inquiry* 1075 (2003).

41 *Hernandez II*, 375, 376 (emphasis in original).

42 *Hernandez v. Robles III* (2006) N.Y. Lexis, 6–7.

43 Ibid., 81.

44 See *Conway v. Deane*, Maryland Case No. 24-C-04-005390.

45 *Kerrigan v. Commissioner of Public Health*, 289 Conn. 135 (2007).

46 Ibid.

47 *Donaldson v. State of Montana*, 292 P.3d 364 (2012), 367 and passim. (A note at the beginning of the opinion states that the pagination for this opinion appears to be out of order but that this numbering sequence replicates the original.)

48 Ibid. 236–237.

49 Ibid., 237.

50 Ibid., 374.

51 Ibid., 371.

52 *Jackson v. Abercrombie*, 884 F. Supp. 2d 1065 (2012), 1072.

53 Lee Edelman, *No Future: Queer Theory and the Death Drive* (Durham, NC: Duke University Press, 2004).

54 See *Elisa B. v. Superior Court*, 37 Cal. 4th 108 (2005); see also *Mariga v. Flint*, 822d N.E. 2d 620 (2005) wherein an Indiana judge, in requiring an adoptive lesbian co-parent to pay child support, reinforced the distinction as follows: "To the contrary, of key importance is the relationship between parent and children, not between parent and parent."

55 Although this latter option is entertained with alarming frequency, it would be difficult (although not unlikely or unexpected) for marriage oppositionists to make a "family values" argument in favor of denying permanent homes to chil-

dren who need them; see *Lofton v. Sec. of Dept. of Children and Family Servs.*, 358 F.3d 804 (2004).

56 *People v. Greenleaf*, 5 Misc. 3d 337 (2004), 342.

57 Valerie Jenness, "Social Movement Growth, Doman Expansion, and Framing Processes: The Gay/Lesbian Movement and Violence against Gays and Lesbians as a Social Problem," 42 *Social Problems* (1995), 145–170.

58 Edelman, *No Future*, 11.

CHAPTER 3. CHILDREN BY THE CARLOAD

1 See, e.g., Judith Butler, *Gender Trouble: Feminism and the Subversion of Identity* (New York: Routledge, 1999); Gayle Rubin, "Thinking Sex: Notes for a Radical Theory of the Politics of Gender," in *The Lesbian and Gay Studies Reader*, ed. Henry Abelove, Michèle Aina Barale, and David M. Halperin (New York: Routledge, 1984).

2 *Baehr v. Lewin*, 74 Haw. 530 (1993), 564–565.

3 Sandi Farrell, "Reconsidering the Gender-Equality Perspective for Understanding LGBT Rights," 13 *Law & Sexuality* 605 (2004), 610.

4 *Skinner v. Oklahoma ex rel. Williamson*, 316 U.S. 535 (1942), 541.

5 *Baehr*, 553.

6 Ibid., 555.

7 Ibid.

8 Jonathan Goldberg-Hiller, *The Limits to Union: Same-Sex Marriage and the Politics of Civil Rights* (Ann Arbor: University of Michigan Press, 2002).

9 *Goodridge v. Dept. of Public Health*, 440 Mass. 309 (2003), 331.

10 Ibid., 331.

11 Ibid., 333.

12 Ibid., 332–333, citation omitted.

13 Ibid., 336.

14 Ibid., 337.

15 Ibid., 337.

16 *In re Marriage Cases*, 143 Cal. App. 4th 873 (2008), 935, footnote 33.

17 Ibid., 962.

18 Ibid., 963.

19 Ibid., 964.

20 Ibid.

21 Ibid., 965.

22 *Kerrigan v. Commissioner of Public Health*, 289 Conn. (2008), 135, 163.

23 Ibid., 141.

24 Ibid., 148.

25 Ibid., 149, citations omitted.

26 Ibid., 151, citations omitted (emphasis in original).

27 Ibid.

28 Ibid., 153, citations omitted.

29 *Baskin v. Bogan*, 766 F.3d 648 (2014), 654.

30 Ibid., 654.
31 Ibid., 657.
32 Ibid., 662.
33 Ibid., 658.
34 Ibid., 657.
35 Ibid., 657–658.
36 Ibid., 663–664.
37 Ibid., 666.
38 Ibid., 667, citation omitted.
39 Ibid.
40 Ibid., 671.
41 Ibid.
42 *Latta v. Otter* (2014) U.S. App. LEXIS 19620, 9.
43 Ibid., 34.
44 Ibid.
45 Ibid., 37.
46 Ibid., 39.
47 Ibid., 41.
48 Ibid., 43.
49 Ibid., 44–45.
50 Ibid., 41.
51 Ibid., 49.
52 Ibid., 56, footnote 2.
53 Katherine Franke, "Sexuality and Marriage: The Politics of Same-Sex Marriage Politics," 15 *Columbia Journal of Gender and Law* 236 (2006).
54 *Latta v. Otter*, 72.
55 Ibid., 85–86, citations omitted.
56 Judge Berzon draws extensively on the scholarly literature about the history of marriage; see George Chauncey, *Why Marriage? The History Shaping Today's Debate over Gay Equality* (New York: Basic Books, 2004); Nancy Cott, "Marriage and Women's Citizenship in the United States, 1830–1934," 103 *American History Review* 1440 (1998); Nancy Cott, *Public Vows: A History of Marriage and the Nation* (Cambridge, MA: Harvard University Press, 2000).
57 *Latta v. Otter*, 94.
58 Ibid., 96–98.
59 Kitty Calavita, "Blue Jeans, Rape and the 'Deconstitutive' Power of Law," 35 *Law & Society Review* (2001).
60 See especially Martha Albertson Fineman, *The Neutered Mother, the Sexual Family, and Other Twentieth Century Tragedies* (New York: Routledge, 1995).

CHAPTER 4. THE NEAREST HIPPIE

1 *United States v. Windsor*, 133 S. Ct. 2675 (2014), 2711.
2 Ibid., 2718.

3 Ibid.
4 Ibid., 2643.
5 *Obergefell v. Hodges*, 135 S. Ct. 2584 (2015), 2629.
6 Ibid., 2613.
7 Ibid.
8 Ibid., 2614.
9 Ibid., 2641.
10 Jonathan Goldberg-Hiller, *The Limits to Union: Same-Sex Marriage and the Politics of Civil Rights* (Ann Arbor: Michigan University Press, 2002), 221.
11 Katherine Franke, *Wedlocked: The Perils of Marriage Equality* (New York: New York University Press, 2015).
12 *Obergefell*, 2626.
13 Ibid., 2627.
14 *Windsor*, 2715.
15 *Obergefell*, 2620.
16 Ibid., 2602.
17 *Windsor*, 2709.
18 Ibid., 2708, citations omitted (emphasis in original).
19 Relevant passages from the *Congressional Record* can be found here: "H.R. 3396—104th Congress: Defense of Marriage Act," GovTrack.us (1996), www.govtrack.us; for an interesting overview of the bill's passage, see indiemcemopants, "Why Was DOMA Enacted?," Daily Kos, March 6, 2011, www.dailykos.com.
20 *Windsor*, 2711.
21 Ibid., 2718.
22 *Obergefell*, 2642.
23 Franke, *Wedlocked*, 12.
24 Ibid., 19.
25 *Lawrence v. Texas*, 539 U.S. 558 (2003), 606.
26 *Obergefell*, 2632.
27 Ibid., 2636.
28 Sora Y. Han, *Letters of the Law: Race and the Fantasy of Colorblindness in American Law* (Stanford, CA: Stanford University Press, 2015).
29 *Obergefell*, 2619.
30 Ibid., 2614–2615.
31 Devon W. Carbado, "Straight Out of the Closet," 15 *Berkeley Women's Law Journal* 76 (2000), 86.
32 Ibid., 105.
33 Dan Savage, *The Kid: What Happened after My Boyfriend and I Decided to Go Get Pregnant* (New York: Penguin Books, 2000).
34 Carbado, "Straight Out of the Closet," 117–122.

CHAPTER 5. A UNION UNLIKE ANY OTHER

1 *United States v. Windsor*, 133 S. Ct. 2675 (2013), 2688.
2 Ibid., 2694.
3 Ibid., 2691–2969.
4 *Obergefell v. Hodges*, 135 S. Ct. 2534 (2015), 2593–2594.
5 Ibid., 2594.
6 Ibid., 2599.
7 Ibid., 2600.
8 Ibid., 2601.
9 Ibid.
10 *Goodridge v. Dept. of Public Health*, 440 Mass. 309 (2003), 334.
11 *Obergefell*, 2601.
12 Ibid., 2594.
13 Ibid., 2606.
14 Ibid.
15 Ibid., 2606–2607, citations omitted.
16 *Windsor*, 2694.
17 Ibid., 2699, 2708.
18 Michael Warner, *The Trouble with Normal: Sex, Politics, and the Ethics of Queer Life* (New York: Free Press, 1999); see also Lisa Duggan, *The Twilight of Equality? Neoliberalism, Cultural Politics, and the Attack on Democracy* (New York: Beacon Press, 1994).
19 Feminist Newswire, "Supreme Court Rules in Favor Marriage Equality," Feminist Majority Foundation, June 26, 2013, feminist.org.
20 *Obergefell*, 2595–2596.
21 Ibid., 2603.
22 Nicola Barker, *Not the Marrying Kind: A Feminist Critique of Same-Sex Marriage* (New York: Palgrave Macmillan, 2013), Kindle Edition loc. 2948.
23 Morris Kaplan, *Sexual Justice: Democratic Citizenship and the Politics of Desire* (New York: Routledge, 1997).
24 Warner, *The Trouble with Normal*; Steven Seidman, "Identity and Politics in a 'Postmodern' Gay Culture: Some Historical and Conceptual Notes," in *Fear of a Queer Planet: Queer Politics and Social Theory*, ed. Michael Warner (Minneapolis: University of Minnesota Press, 1993).
25 Nancy Polikoff, "We Will Get What We Ask For: Why Legalizing Gay and Lesbian Marriage Will Not 'Dismantle the Legal Structure of Gender in Every Marriage,'" 79 *Virginia Law Rev.* 1535 (1993).
26 Katherine Franke, "Sexuality and Marriage: The Politics of Same-Sex Marriage Politics," 15 *Columbia Journal of Gender and Law* 236 (2006), 246.
27 Ibid.
28 J. Jack Halberstam, *In a Queer Time and Place: Transgender Bodies, Subcultural Lives* (New York: New York University Press, 2005).

29 Philippe Ariès, *Centuries of Childhood: A Social History of Family Life* (New York: Vintage Books, 1965); Kathryn Bond Stockton, *The Queer Child, or Growing Sideways in the Twentieth Century* (Durham, NC: Duke University Press, 2009).

30 Lee Edelman, *No Future: Queer Theory and the Death Drive* (Durham, NC: Duke University Press, 2004), 11.

31 *Obergefell*, 2606.

32 Ibid., 2598.

CONCLUSION

1 Jane Ward, *Not Gay: Sex Between Straight White Men* (New York: New York University Press, 2016).

2 J. Jack Halberstam, *The Queer Art of Failure* (Durham, NC: Duke University Press, 2011), 70.

3 Ibid., 69.

4 *Parker v. Hurley*, 474 F. Supp. 2d 261 (2007), 263

5 Ibid.

6 Judith Butler, "Is Kinship Always Already Heterosexual?," in *Left Liberalism/Left Critique*, ed. Wendy Brown and Janet Halley (Durham, NC: Duke University Press, 2002); Janet Halley, "The Construction of Heterosexuality," in *Fear of a Queer Planet: Queer Politics and Social Theory*, ed. Michael Warner (Minneapolis: University of Minnesota Press, 1993); Gayle Rubin, "Thinking Sex: Notes for a Radical Theory of the Politics of Sexuality," in Henry Abelove, et al., *The Lesbian and Gay Studies Reader*, ed. Henry Abelove, Michèle Aina Barale, and David M. Halperin (New York: Routledge, 1993).

7 *Parker*, 278.

8 Yesonprop8, "Proposition 8 Commercial," October 25, 2008; the ad can be found at www.youtube.com.

9 Allaymennay, "No on Prop 8: A Family Speaks Out," October 23, 2008; the ad can be found at www.youtube.com.

10 Joe Rollins, "Sexting Cyberchildren: Gender, Sexuality, and Childhood in Social Media and Law," 19, no. 1 *Sexuality & Culture* (2015).

11 Jessica Ringrose, Laura Harvey, Rosalind Gill, and Sonia Livingstone, "Teen Girls, Sexual Double Standards and 'Sexting': Gendered Value in Digital Image Exchange," 14 *Feminist Theory* 305 (2013).

12 Michel Foucault, *The History of Sexuality: An Introduction, Volume I* (New York: Vintage Books, 1978); Halley, "The Construction of Heterosexuality"; Eve Kosofsky Sedgwick, *Epistemology of the Closet* (Berkeley: University of California Press, 1990); Ward, *Not Gay*.

13 Michele Goodwin, "Fetal Protection Laws: Moral Panic and the New Constitutional Battlefront," 102 *California Law Review* 781 (2014), citations omitted.

14 Utah State Legislature, "S.B. 234: Protecting Unborn Children Amendments" (2016); the text of the bill can be found at le.utah.gov.

15 Linda Greenhouse, "The Abortion Map Today," *New York Times*, April 13, 2016.
16 Erik Eckholm, "Oklahoma Passes Bill That Would Subject Abortion Doctors to Felony Charges," *New York Times*, May 19, 2016.
17 Sabrina Tavernise and Sheryl Gay Stolberg, "Abortion Foes, Emboldened by Trump, Promise 'Onslaught' of New Restrictions," *New York Times*, December 11, 2016; Lizette Alvarez, "Texas Again Places Obstacles in Front of Those Seeking Abortions," *New York Times*, December 1, 2016.
18 *Planned Parenthood of Wisconsin v. Schimel*, 806 F3d 908 (2015), 916, citations omitted.
19 *Whole Woman's Health v. Hellerstedt*, No. 15-274 (Slip Op.) (2016).
20 Brian Ross, Rhonda Schwartz, and John Capell, "Exclusive: Alleged Dennis Hastert Sex Abuse Victim Named by Family," ABC News, June 5, 2015; video can be found at abcnews.go.com.
21 Jessica Hopper, "Jaycee Dugard Interview: She Describes Giving Birth in Phillip Garrido's Backyard Prison," ABC News, July 7, 2011; the complete interview can be seen at abcnews.go.com.
22 Jeffrey Toobin, "The Celebrity Defense: Sex, Fame, and the Case of Roman Polanski," *New Yorker*, December 14, 2009.
23 Dylan Farrow, "An Open Letter from Dylan Farrow," *New York Times*, February 1, 2014. This text was taken from Nicholas Kristof's blog, where the letter was published: kristof.blogs.nytimes.com.
24 Tom Zito, "In the Land of Dreams and Eternal Youth, Bizarre Events Are Nothing New," *Washington Post*, March 26, 1977, www.washingtonpost.com.
25 Rebecca Keegan, "Samantha Geimer Tells Her Side of Story in Roman Polanski Case," *Los Angeles Times*, September 16, 2013, articles.latimes.com.
26 Farrow, "An Open Letter from Dylan Farrow." Nicholas Kristof introduces the letter with text of his own.
27 Ibid.
28 Ibid.
29 See, e.g., Foucault, *History of Sexuality*; Peter Hegarty, *Gentlemen's Disagreement: Alfred Kinsey, Lewis Terman, and the Sexual Politics of Smart Men* (Chicago: University of Chicago Press, 2013); Rubin, "Thinking Sex"; Warner, *Fear of a Queer Planet*.
30 Office of the Provost, Harvard University, "Title IX and Gender Equity" (2015). Harvard's Title IX policy can be found at titleix.harvard.edu.
31 Laura Kipnis, "Sexual Paranoia Strikes Academe," *Chronicle of Higher Education: The Chronicle Review*, February 27, 2015.
32 Laura Kipnis, "My Title IX Inquisition," *Chronicle of Higher Education: The Chronicle Review*, May 29, 2015.
33 Dave Philipps, "North Carolina Bans Local Anti-discrimination Policies," *New York Times*, March 24, 2016, www.nytimes.com.
34 Samantha Allen, "Mississippi's Anti-LGBT Law Is Worse Than North Carolina's," *Daily Beast*, March 31, 2016, www.thedailybeast.com.

35 Mississippi House Bill 1523; the text can be found at http://billstatus.ls.state.ms.us/documents/2016/html/HB/1500-1599/HB1523SG.htm.
36 Nick Gass, "Transgender Bathroom Battle Rocks Republican Race," *Politico*, April 21, 2016, www.politico.com.
37 "Woman Marches through Target Blasting Transgender Bathroom Policy," May 18, 2016, www.foxnews.com.
38 Alain de Botton, "Why You Will Marry the Wrong Person," *New York Times*, May 28, 2016, www.nytimes.com.
39 Eve Kosofsky Sedgwick, *Epistemology of the Closet* (Berkeley: University of California Press, 1990).

INDEX

ABOUT THE AUTHOR

Joe Rollins is Professor of Political Science at Queens College and the Graduate Center, CUNY. His research interests emphasize gender and sexuality as they are negotiated in the American legal system. He has also served as Co-editor of *Women's Studies Quarterly.*